THE
EMPLOYEE EXPERIENCE ADVANTAGE

THE

EMPLOYEE EXPERIENCE ADVANTAGE

HOW TO WIN THE WAR FOR TALENT BY GIVING EMPLOYEES THE WORKSPACES THEY WANT, THE TOOLS THEY NEED, AND A CULTURE THEY CAN CELEBRATE

JACOB MORGAN

WILEY

Published by John Wiley & Sons, Inc., Hoboken, New Jersey

Published simultaneously in Canada

Library of Congress Cataloging-in-Publication Data is Available:

9781119321620 (Hardcover)
9781119321651 (ePDF)
9781119321637 (epub)

Cover Design: Wiley
Cover Image: © Gerard Allen Mendoza

Printed in the United States of America

10 9 8 7 6 5 4 3 2 1

To Naomi, welcome to the world. I will do my best to create as many amazing experiences for you as I can. To my wife, Blake, you are my everything and I love you!

Contents

Foreword

As an executive coach, I have worked with some remarkable leaders – people with outstanding achievements and unbelievable wealth. Any outsider would assume they were happy.

They'd be wrong. Even these fortunate people often struggle to find happiness. Like so many others, they succumb to the great Western disease—I will be happy *when*. When I get promoted. When I reach the next professional milestone. When I make a certain amount of money. In reality, while it feels good to buy a fancy car or get the corner office, that joy wears off pretty fast. That's why I tell my clients not to hold out for prizes. Be happy now.

Jacob Morgan understands this fundamental truth—which is one reason I find this book so compelling. He makes a strong case for the value of jobs that create happiness, satisfaction, and well-being *in the present*.

He's right that extrinsic rewards (like pay or bonuses) don't really motivate workers. Once they reach a certain baseline salary, money is no longer the main driver. They need something more. Reams have been written about the Millennial generation's hunger for impact and meaning at work. In one way, I think Millennials (and Generation Z, coming up after them) are not so different from the rest of us. They just voice desires the rest of us have learned to keep quiet.

We don't want to suffer through an unpleasant job so that we can get a reward on payday, or when we at long last reach retirement—especially now that the borders of the workday are blurring. With flexible work arrangements and technology that follows us home after the workday has officially ended, our personal and professional lives are no longer truly separate. If we wait until work is over to start accruing satisfying and meaningful experiences, we might end up waiting an awfully long time.

In my seminars, I argue that employees don't have to depend on a boss or an organization to make their working lives better. They can bring about positive change all by themselves. I recommend a process called the Daily Questions, which involves asking yourself a series of questions every day to see how much effort you put toward your main priorities. (I pay a colleague to call me every day for this very reason!) This way, the individual can be an agent of change, creating meaning, happiness and engagement from within.

Employees can engage themselves much better than an HR program can. And yet it's in the interest of organizations to improve levels of employee engagement, so they try. Given the stiff competition for top talent, it's easy to see why. Yet the billions they've invested haven't yielded much, as Morgan rightly notes. His explanation: they are looking at effects (engagement) without causes (the experiences that lead to certain levels of engagement). He recommends focusing on the root cause: the technological, physical, and cultural environments around the employee.

By looking closely at how environments affect workers, he offers some fresh and timely perspective. Most of us go through life unaware of how powerfully our environments shape our behavior. Because of another Western predilection to assume that we are in control—of ourselves and of our circumstances—we often fail to see that our environments rule us instead of the other way around.

My book *Triggers: Creating Behavior That Lasts, Becoming the Person You Want to Be* (with Mark Reiter; Crown, 2015) explores our triggers—the people and situations that often lure us into behaving in a manner unlike the colleague, partner, parent, or friend we hope and imagine ourselves to be. These triggers are relentless, constant, and omnipresent. The smell of bacon wafts up from the kitchen, and we forget our doctor's advice on lowering our cholesterol. Our phone chirps, and we glance instinctively at the glowing screen instead of looking into the eyes of the person we're with. Without a plan or a structured approach, these distractions can easily send our careers and lives off course.

Environmental triggers have profound implications in the workplace, which Morgan explores in admirable depth. His research reveals what cutting-edge companies are doing to create environments that are helpful and stimulating, instead of taxing and draining. He has done his homework, and as a result he's able to show a wide range of fascinating new ideas and strategies. Whether you connect with all of them or just a few of them, this book is worth a read for the insight into what the future portends.

In our age of rapid technological advancement and unprecedented volatility, the only true certainty is change. *The Employee Experience* will arm leaders and organizations with future-focused intelligence about how to get great people and keep them inspired and motivated.

Marshall Goldsmith

Acknowledgments

When I wrote *The Collaborative Organization*, I was engaged. When I wrote my second book, *The Future of Work*, I was married. Now, with *The Employee Experience Advantage*, I'm a dad.

Each book thus far has been accompanied by a major life event and amazing new experiences. I am grateful for all of them and am excited to see what will happen when I write my next book!

My wife, Blake, has been my biggest source of inspiration, encouragement, and support. We spend most of our time together working and playing, and I'm so fortunate to have married my best friend. She makes me a better person. My family both near and far, I love you very much and appreciate your continued support and curiosity for what I do!

Writing a book is certainly a journey, and this one has been no exception, especially when considering the extensive research project that was conducted. I want to thank the John Wiley & Sons team for helping make this book possible: Lia, Peter, Shannon, and Elizabeth, you have all been a pleasure to work with (again!). Serge da Motta Veiga from American University, thank you for your support and guidance during the launch of this project. Steve King from Emergent Research, your advice, e-mails, and phone calls really helped shape this project; thank you so much for your brilliant insights. Connie Chan, my business partner at The Future of Work Community, thank you for your continued support. A big thank-you to all the members of The Future of Work Community, who continue to graciously share insights, ideas, and interesting topics for me to explore and think about. I've interviewed hundreds of senior executives at organizations around the world; thanks to all of you for being so open and transparent with me.

A big thank-you to my team, who do an awesome job supporting me. Allen Mendoza, you're the best creative designer I have ever worked with; thank you for creating the book jacket and all the images in this book! Megan and Jen, thanks for keeping me on track and organized and

for all you do to help make sure my ideas and messages keep spreading!
Vlada, many thousands of people have listened to my podcasts and videos
that you helped put together; thank you. Trisa, Teresa, Stacy, Alexis, and
Erica, thanks for helping me research the hundreds of companies for this
research project. Jeffrey, you are an awesome data scientist and analyst.
Thank you for the hundreds of hours you contributed to help make sure
all the collected data was accurate, reliable, and something that I could
actually understand!

Two organizations graciously agreed to sponsor the research that
is shared throughout this book. Those two organizations are Lever
and Cisco, which you will learn more about in the following chapters.
Francine Katsoudas, Gianpaolo Barozzi, and Leela Srinivasan, thanks
for your continued support and for believing in me and in this project!

We All Care about Experience (Introduction)

Life is short, very short. We might as well make the most of it while we have it. This is why so many of us want to explore the world, try new things, and otherwise venture off the beaten path, because as humans we are by nature curious. This is also why many of us focus on creating experiences instead of simply owning material things. We save up to eat at fancy restaurants on special occasions, go skydiving, visit exotic cities thousands of miles away from where we live, climb mountains, and do all sorts of other experiential activities. Nobody makes us do these things; we do them because we want to, all for the sake of getting that experience that will hopefully last us a long time or a lifetime. Most people don't stop to think about it, but experiences are really one of the main things that make us human.

Research done by Cornell University psychology professor Dr. Thomas Gilovich, University of Chicago postdoctoral research fellow Dr. Amit Kumar, and Dr. Matthew Killingsworth, who studies human happiness at the University of California, San Francisco, found that when people spend their money on experiences, over time their satisfaction goes up whereas when people spend money on physical things, over time their satisfaction goes down. The research also found that waiting for an experience elicits more happiness than waiting for a material good. Finally, they found when we spend money on experiences, those purchases are also more associated with our identity, connection, and social behavior. People who spend money on experiences instead of things are just happier all around.

In the past year, how many times have you spent your time or money on creating experiences for yourself or for others? A hundred times? Fifty times? What about in the past six months or the past week? What about in the past 24 hours? I'm willing to bet that you spend quite a bit of time and money on creating experiences regularly. Experiences stay with us throughout our lives. Not only do they shape who we are as human beings, but also they help us connect with and build relationships with others.

Clearly we as human beings care about experiences because we are willing to spend our hard-earned time and money on creating them. We don't do this simply for the experiences themselves and for the feelings we get during a particular moment but because they create memories. The experiences themselves may be ephemeral, but the memories they create last far longer. So if experiences are so vital to our existence as human beings, then what happened to experience inside of our organizations? When you consider that we spend about 30 percent of our entire lives working (assuming you work only 40 hours a week, which many of us go far beyond) this becomes a scary statistic. We can even take this one step further and ask, "What happened to the humanity inside our organizations?" These experiences and their subsequent memories help shape the type of relationship we want (or don't want) to have with a coworker, manager, or organization as a whole.

As the world becomes more fascinated with discussions of robots and automation, this experience aspect is more important than ever! While many futurists and business leaders believe that robots and automation are taking jobs away from humans, I believe that it's the humans who are taking the jobs away from robots.

Decades ago before the Internet, when modern management was just getting started, we didn't have any type of connectivity, and these discussions around robots and automation weren't even an afterthought. It was perhaps a much simpler time when the role of humans was simply to show up at the same time every day, do the same job over and over, wear the same outfit or uniform, report to the same person, take a break at the same time, not ask any questions or cause any problems, and work like a robot basically. But we didn't have robots or automation at the time so what did we do? We used humans. Basically we have designed perfect organizations for robots and automation, but because we didn't have those at the time, we used the next best thing: people. Now, when these technologies finally exist, they are claiming the jobs and responsibilities that we designed for them to begin with. Humans were simply placeholders like bookmarks in a novel. Today organizations around the world are trying to figure out how they have to redesign themselves to focus more on people . . . more on humans. Robots don't care about experiences at work but humans do.

The experiences organizations design are ultimately what shape the actions that employees take and the relationships or associations that they want to have with your organization (if any). The challenge we have to overcome today is how to shift our relationship with work from feeling like a physical purchase, where satisfaction starts to decline over time, to an investment in an experience, where our satisfaction increases over time.

This is further supported with research done by career website Glassdoor. On its blog Mario Nuñez posted an article titled "Does Money Buy Happiness? The Link Between Salary and Employee Satisfaction," which revealed something quite surprising. According to the article:

> One unexpected finding is that there is a clear relationship between years of experience and happiness at work. In short, older workers tend to be less satisfied. For example, a one-year increase in years of experience is associated with a 0.6-point decrease in overall employee satisfaction, after controlling for all other factors. This might reflect learning about the quality of work environments over time. Or perhaps workers become more jaded with their employer as they progress throughout their career.[1]

This was based on a sample of 221,000 Glassdoor users.

In my last book, *The Future of Work* (Wiley, 2014), I shared that synonyms for *employee* include *cog*, *servant*, and *slave*; synonyms for *manager* include *boss*, *slave driver*, and *zookeeper*. Synonyms for *work* include *drudgery*, *struggle*, and *daily grind*. This is quite literally how we have structured many of our organizations over the past few decades. We have actually designed the humanity out of our organizations. However, today we are starting to realize that this way of thinking about work no longer makes any sense.

The one big assumption we have always had about our organizations has now proven to be completely wrong. Organizations have always assumed that people needed to work there. After all, you have expenses, bills to pay, a family to look after, and things you want to buy. The organization has a job it can offer you to help you take care of those things so it's clearly a good fit. This has been the traditional relationship between employer and employee, and organizations have always had all the control and the power. Again this was the simple equivalent of purchasing a physical good. Oftentimes these same organizations were simply able to rely on their brand power to attract and retain talent.

Today that is no longer the case. The war for talent has never been fiercer, and in an effort to attract and retain the best and brightest, organizations have to shift from creating places where they assume people need to be to creating organizations where people truly want to be. This shift in approach from need to want is also causing organizations to move from utility to employee experience.

NOTE

1. Nuñez, Mario. "Does Money Buy Happiness? The Link Between Salary and Employee Satisfaction." *Glassdoor Economic Research Blog*, June 18, 2015. https://www.glassdoor.com/research/does-money-buy-happiness-the-link-between-salary-and-employee-satisfaction/.

PART I
The Evolution of Employee Experience

As with anything in the business world, things evolve and change. The evolution that we are seeing today continues to shift organizational priorities more and more toward focusing on people and bringing humanity and experiences into our organizations. This is an immensely exciting thing to see! Years ago with the advent of what many would consider modern business, focusing on utility,that is, the basic components of work,made sense. At the time, it was just common practice, and pretty much every organization took the same approach. Then, this shifted toward productivity, getting the most out of people. Next, we saw the emergence of engagement, which is all about making employees happy and engaged at work. Now, we are shifting to what I believe is the next and most important area of organizational design, employee experience. Let's look at this evolution and how we got to where we are.

CHAPTER 1

Defining Employee Experience

UTILITY

Decades ago the relationship we had with our employers was pretty straightforward. Employers had jobs they needed to fill; we had bills to pay, things we wanted to buy, and certain skills we could offer, so we tried to get that open job. This basic relationship also meant that work was always about utility, that is, the bare-bones, essential tools and resources that an employer can provide employees to get their jobs done (see Figure 1.1). Today that is typically a computer, desk, cubicle, and phone. In the past this may have been a desk, pen, notepad, and phone, or perhaps just a hammer and nails. That was it. Can you imagine if someone were to bring up health and wellness programs, catered meals, bringing dogs to the office, or flexible work efforts in the past? Give me a break! They would be laughed at and the employee most likely fired on the spot! These things are all relatively new phenomena that are now only starting to gain global attention and investment. Granted, there are still plenty of organizations out there that are still stuck in the utility world.

PRODUCTIVITY

After the utility era came the productivity era. This is where folks like Frederick Winslow Taylor and Henri Fayol pioneered methods and

Utility

What do employees need to work?

✓ Bare-bones tools
✓ Desk, chair, phone, and computer
✓ Employee is truly a cog

Productivity

What do employees need to work better and faster?

✓ Slight improvements to get more out of people
✓ Employee optimization
✓ Repeatable processes

Engagement

How can we make employees happy so they perform better?

✓ Annual survey
✓ Focus on culture
✓ Acts as adrenaline shot
✓ Company has a mission statement

Experience

How can we create a company where people want to show up vs. need to show up?

✓ Focus on culture, technology, and space
✓ Purposeful design
✓ Long-term approach
✓ Company has a reason for being

JACOB MORGAN

© thefutureorganization.com

FIGURE 1.1 Evolution of Employee Experience

approaches to optimize how employees worked. Managers literally used stopwatches to time how long it would take employees to complete a task to shave off a few seconds here and there. It was analogous to trying to get a sprinter or swimmer to improve his or her lap time. All of this was designed to improve productivity and output while emphasizing repeatable processes, such as the famous factory assembly line. Unfortunately at the time, we didn't have robots and automation to do these jobs (which they would have been perfect for), so instead we used humans. Today, we finally have the technology capable to do the jobs they were designed for, and the humans who were simply acting as placeholders are now in trouble. Robots aren't taking jobs away from humans; it's the humans who took the jobs away from robots. As with the utility era, there also wasn't much focus on creating an organization where the employee truly wanted to be. Productivity was simply utility on steroids!

ENGAGEMENT

Next came engagement, a radically new concept where we saw the collective business world say, "Hey, maybe we should pay more attention to employees and what they care about and value instead of just trying to extract more from them." And thus, the era of engagement (or enlightenment) was born. This was actually quite a revolutionary approach that shifted some of the focus away from how the organization can benefit and extract more value from employees to focusing on what the organization can do to benefit the employees and understand how and why they work. The more engaged an employee is, the better! This is where we stopped and where we have been for the past two or three decades. There have been all sorts of studies that have shown engaged employees are more productive, stay at the company longer, and are generally healthier and happier.

I'll admit that when I first started writing this book, I was convinced that employee experience and engagement were at odds with each other. I mistakenly believed that experience must replace engagement. In fact there were thousands of words originally devoted to that very rationale that I had to scrap from this book. I've since changed my tune. Employee experience doesn't need to replace engagement. The two can actually work together, and in fact, they have to. Instead I view employee experience as something that creates engaged employees but focuses on the cultural, technological, and physical design of the organization to do that. Still, our current definitions and understanding of employee engagement need to evolve before that can happen. Many of the questions and frameworks used to explore engagement haven't changed since they were first introduced into the business world, which creates some challenges.

EMPLOYEE EXPERIENCE

Let's say you buy an old car at a junkyard and then spend thousands of dollars on new paint, upholstery, rims, and interior upgrades. Even though the car will look beautiful, it will still drive like the same car you brought home from the junkyard. If you want to improve how the car performs, then you need to replace the engine. Organizations around the world are investing considerable resources into things such as corporate culture programs, office redesigns, employee engagement initiatives, and well-being strategies. Unfortunately these things make the organization look better but have little impact on how it actually performs.

Many organizations today use *employee engagement* and *employee experience* interchangeably without any distinguishable difference, which is incorrect. Employee engagement has been all about short-term cosmetic changes that organizations have been trying to make to improve how they work. If this approach doesn't work for a car, then it certainly won't work for an organization.

If employee engagement is the short-term adrenaline shot, then employee experience is the long-term redesign of the organization. It's the focus on the engine instead of on the paint and upholstery. Chances are you've heard of the term *customer experience*, which is typically defined as "the relationship that a customer has with a brand." Most people reading that would say, "Well, of course that's what it is. Isn't that obvious?" Yes it is, which is why I think it's really a meaningless definition that provides no context or direction for what that actually looks like. This is why I wanted to avoid simply defining *employee experience* as "the relationship between an employee and the organization." That doesn't help anyone or provide any value, and as with the customer experience, it's rather obvious. So then what is employee experience?

There are a few ways we must look at this. The first is through the eyes of the employee, the second is through the eyes of the organization, and the third is the overlap between the two. When reading through these you may decide to lean toward the side of the employee or the organization, but since two parties are involved, it is in both the employee's and the organization's best interest if we view employee experience as something that is created and affected by both.

For the people who are a part of your organization, their experience is simply the reality of what it's like to work there. From the perspective of the organization, employee experience is what is designed and created for employees, or put another way, it's what the organization believes the employee reality should be like. This, of course, is a challenge and one we see in our everyday lives. Have you ever said or done something to a loved one or friend that was well intentioned yet was perceived as being rude or disrespectful? This is the same scenario we see play out between organizations and employees all the time. Just because the organization does something doesn't mean the employees perceive it in the intended way. Naturally this causes problems not just in our personal lives but also at work.

You may have seen *The Truman Show*, a film about a man who is living in a world that was designed for him by an organization. His entire perceived world was constructed from a massive stage, and although he didn't realize it, every action and event that took place was planned. Regardless of how hard the organization tried to keep Truman from leaving the world that was created for him, he eventually did break free. In some ways this is how our organizations operate. They tell us when we can work, what tools we should use, what to wear, when we can get promoted or learn something new, whom we can talk to, and when we can eat or take breaks. Not only that but they also control the environments we work in and pretty much anything and everything else that happens within the walls of the organization. As an employee you have virtually no say in what happens for around 8 to 10 hours of your day. Although our organizations aren't exactly Truman-izing our lives, there are parallels that can be drawn here. So where does that leave us?

The ideal scenario is the overlap between the employee's reality and the organization's design of that employee reality. In other words, the organization designs or does something, and the employees perceive it in the intended way. This is possible because as you will see in the following chapters, employees actually help shape their experiences instead of simply having them designed by the organization (aka the Truman approach).

Taking that viewpoint, one can define employee experience as "the intersection of employee expectations, needs, and wants and the organizational design of those expectations, needs, and wants." You can see this in Figure 1.2 below.

FIGURE 1.2   Employee Experience Design

However, what resonates more with people is saying "designing an organization where people want to show up by focusing on the cultural, technological, and physical environments." Phrasing it this way essentially encapsulates the entire relationship and journey that an employee experiences while interacting with an organization, but it also breaks it down a bit into three distinct environments, which makes it easier to understand than saying, "Employee experience is everything."

One crucial thing to keep in mind is that employee experiences can't be created unless the organization knows its employees. The word *organization* is broadly used as a way to represent executives, managers, and the collective workforce. If you've ever booked a trip through a travel agent, you know that he or she spends an extensive amount of time getting to know who you are. That way he or she can plan a trip for you that is sure to give you a memorable experience. In the same way that travel agents truly know who their customers are, the organization must truly know who its workforce is. As you will see later in this book, that means not only leveraging people analytics but also having a team of leaders who have the capacity and the desire to connect with people on a truly individual and human level.

Experience is also subjective because human beings have emotions, different perceptions, attitudes, and behaviors. If we all behaved the same way and thought the same way, then it would be quite easy for organizations to design perfect employee experiences all the time for everyone. Of course, this is not the case. Does this mean that organizations should simply give up? Clearly not. As you will see in this book, employee experiences are made up of a specific set of environments and variables, and the leading organizations have invested considerable time and resources into making sure they are implemented properly. Every organization in the world has employees who have their own experiences. Whether you help create them or not, they still exist. Employee experience is simply too important and too key of a business differentiator simply to be left up to chance.

As I mentioned earlier, though, this employee experience design process isn't just done for employees; it's done with them. That's a very important point to keep in mind because many organizations get stuck in the *design for* mentality, which kills their efforts.

The majority of this book will explore how to design and create employee experiences by building what I call the Experiential Organization. Let's define what this actually means:

An Experiential Organization (ExpO) is one that has been (re)designed to truly know its people and has mastered the art and science of creating a place where people want, not need, to show up to work. The Experiential Organization does this by creating a Reason for Being and by focusing on the physical, technological, and cultural environments.

From here on out we will take a deep dive into what these environments are, the variables that shape them, and how to go about creating an Experiential Organization that outperforms the competition.

CHAPTER 2

Research on Employee Experience

I certainly didn't coin the term *employee experience*, but I did create the frameworks and approaches that you will find in this book. As far as I'm aware, I'm the only one to create a structured framework of employee experience that is based on actual data and organizational analysis of hundreds of organizations, so it only makes sense to share how it all came about. Although new titles, roles, and practice areas are emerging around employee experience regularly, there's a lot of confusion and uncertainty about what this actually is and what it looks like. Part of the reason for this is unlike traditional human resources (HR), which is very clearly defined, employee experience looks quite different depending on the organization, and that's okay. Because this is a very human-centric role, there should naturally be differences in how various organizations approach this. I reached out to many chief employee experience officers, directors, managers, and even HR leaders who are responsible for employee experience to get their perspective on what this new shift is all about.

Many business executives and leaders I talked to were very candid and said they weren't entirely sure what this role focused on, what experience will become, or even what it will include because it's so new. Naturally this presented me a bit of a challenge in writing a book about this topic. Over the past two years I've had a few hundred conversations with senior executives and employees at various levels. Although I received many responses when I asked, "What makes up employee experience?" or "How do you design employee experiences?" a pattern started to emerge that allowed me to break this down. I started to see that every organization around the world regardless of size, industry, or location was investing in and focusing on three areas, which I like to think of as environments. The environments that affect employee experience are the technological environment, physical environment, and cultural environment.

Once I determined these three environments, the next step was to figure out what the major attributes were within these environments. In other words, what do employees care about most that create great technological, physical, and cultural environments?

This wasn't an easy task because we all care about and value different things. I took the same approach I used with determining the three experience environments. I looked for patterns in the many studies, articles, and research reports I read and added information from the hundreds of conversations I've had with executives and employees at organizations around the world. Based on that I created a series of questions to measure organizational effectiveness in each of the three employee experience environments.

To design great employee experiences and to create a place where employees truly want to show up, organizations must focus on a Reason for Being followed by 17 attributes that are abbreviated as ACE technology, COOL physical spaces, and a CELEBRATED culture (see Figure 2.1).

What I found especially fascinating is that every one of these 17 attributes positively affects the employees and the organization as a whole. This isn't one sided so even by investing in the overall success of the company, the employee experience is also hugely affected positively. Everyone wins.

Together these 17 attributes make up what I like to call the Employee Experience Score (ExS). You can get your organization's EXS by answering the questions that appear in the Appendix. The collective rankings of the organizations that I evaluated then comprise the Employee Experience Index (EEI). You can see the full index as well as get your own EXS by visiting https://TheFutureOrganization.com.

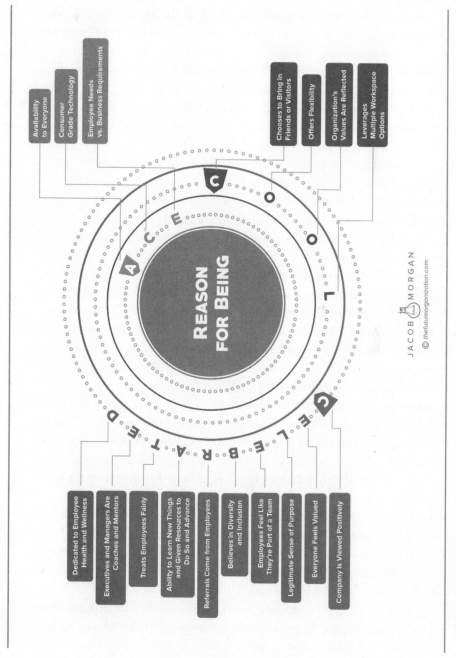

FIGURE 2.1 The 17 Employee Experience Attributes

Availability to Everyone

Consumer Grade Technology

Employee Needs vs. Business Requirements

Chooses to Bring in Friends or Visitors

Offers Flexibility

Organization's Values Are Reflected

Leverages Multiple Workspace Options

REASON FOR BEING

Dedicated to Employee Health and Wellness

Executives and Managers Are Coaches and Mentors

Treats Employees Fairly

Ability to Learn New Things and Given Resources to Do So and Advance

Referrals Come from Employees

Believes in Diversity and Inclusion

Employees Feel Like They're Part of a Team

Legitimate Sense of Purpose

Everyone Feels Valued

Company Is Viewed Positively

JACOB MORGAN

© thefutureorganization.com

To come up with these attributes and the model of employee experience, I:

- Interviewed C-level executives and business leaders at over 150 organizations around the world, including:
  - the chief human resources officer (CHRO) of LinkedIn,
  - CHRO of Accenture
  - the CHRO of Marriott International
  - management professor Marshall Goldsmith
  - the chief technology officer of Xerox
  - the co-CEO of Gensler
  - the chief diversity and inclusion officer at SAP
  - the chief economist at General Electric
  - the chief people officer of Cisco
  - the chief information officer of IBM
  - the chairman of the board at Yahoo!
  - the president of Infosys, and many others
- Reviewed over 150 research articles on culture, technology, and the physical work environment from the likes of Genser, Deloitte, Aon, Steelcase, government agencies, *Harvard Business Review*, and *MIT Sloan Management Review*
- Read dozens of media publications
- Analyzed over 250 organizations, including the Fortune 100, *Fortune's* 100 Best Places to Work, the Glassdoor Best Places to Work, and others
- Worked with an academic institution (American University, with Serge P. da Motta Veiga, assistant professor of management) to help structure the survey and get advice about data collection
- Brought on a research advisor (Steve King from Emergent Research) to provide overall project guidance
- Developed a team of executives to review the attributes and provide feedback and suggestions on the survey

Based on the research conducted for this book, the cultural environment contributes 40 percent to the employee experience, and the technological and physical environments each contribute 30 percent. The total possible score that an organization can receive is 115.5, with 19.5 points coming from technology, 26 points from physical space, and 70 points from culture. Note that the point allocation doesn't reflect the percentage allocated to each environment.

I encourage organizations to take the methodologies in this book and apply them internally. While I don't claim to have all the answers, I do believe that what I have been able to put together does provide some valuable insights into what employee experience is, why it's crucial, and how to go about designing employee experience to create an organization where people actually want to be.

A NOTE ABOUT THE RESEARCH SPONSORS

Two organizations were instrumental in enabling me to conduct the research required for this book. As you can imagine, hiring a team of researchers and data scientists to review 252 organizations can be quite a resource-intensive task. Lever and Cisco were the two cosponsors of my research. Lever is best described as a modern recruiting technology that dramatically simplifies the hiring and applicant tracking process. I met with Leela Srinivasan, the chief marketing officer of Lever, in its San Francisco office when I started writing this book. She was intrigued with the research and decided to support it. Cisco is the world's leading IT company on a mission to help connect everyone and everything. I've been fortunate to have a relationship with Cisco that has spanned a few years. After hearing what I wanted to do, Francine Katsoudas, Cisco's chief people officer, and Gianpaolo Barozzi, Cisco's senior director of HR, agreed to sponsor this research. I'm grateful to both Lever and Cisco for believing in this concept and for wanting to shed more light on employee experience. Both of these organizations had no say, influence, input, or decision-making ability of any kind on any aspect of the research to make sure it remained 100 percent objective.

CHAPTER 3

Employee Experience Drivers

You might be wondering why employee experience is gaining traction just now. After all, customer experience has been around for decades, so why has it taken so long for organizations to look inward? Not only that but we've also been talking about employee engagement for decades as well. Clearly there is something going on that is creating this shift, forcing organizations not only to create new titles and roles but also to actually redesign the way they are structured and how they operate. In my previous book, *The Future of Work*, I explored five trends shaping the future of work, which I will briefly outline here:

1. **Mobility:** Access to people and information anytime, anywhere, and on any device
2. **Millennials and changing demographics:** In addition to the five-generation workforce, organizations are struggling to adapt to an entirely new generation of millennials.
3. **Technology:** Big data, wearables, the Internet of things, AI, and automation are just some of the new technologies organizations are trying to figure out.
4. **New behaviors:** Thanks to social technologies, we are all comfortable living a more public life where we share ideas and information for the world to see.

5. **Globalization:** The world itself is becoming like one big city where the boundaries and barriers to doing any type of business are disappearing.

These five trends are still very relevant today from a broader perspective. However, when looking specifically at employee experience, we need to pay attention to a few other things.

POOR SUCCESS WITH ENGAGEMENT

There are all sorts of associations, institutes, and surveys that organizations can use to measure and look at employee engagement. Unfortunately with all the talk of engagement and with all the trainings and rankings of organizations around the world, engagement has remained relatively unchanged despite our collective investments. According to Gallup, which has become the global authority on this topic, worldwide employee engagement is at 13 percent,[1] which is almost unimaginably low. Perhaps what's more shocking is that this number has barely budged in years! Interestingly enough Aon has global employee engagement at 65 percent for 2016, with a 3 percent improvement since 2014.[2] The fact that these numbers are so far away from each other is another matter entirely.

This is quite an interesting paradox. Engagement has become one of the key focus areas for organizations around the world, and the growth in the industry has never been stronger. Yet somehow the numbers aren't budging. How can that be the case?

There are a few issues I see with focusing on employee engagement and you might have identified others.

Engagement Measures Downward

Let's look at one of the most popular engagement models in the world today. This particular framework categorizes three types of employees:

1. **Actively disengaged:** unhappy employees who undermine their coworkers

2. **Not engaged:** employees who are checked out and sleepwalking through their jobs
3. **Engaged:** employees who work with passion, feel connected to the company, and help move the organization forward

In this model which you can see in figure 3.1, an engaged employee should be the minimum of what an organization should expect from anyone. If we're being honest, then it's fair to say that an engaged employee should be an average employee. In grading terms this would be a

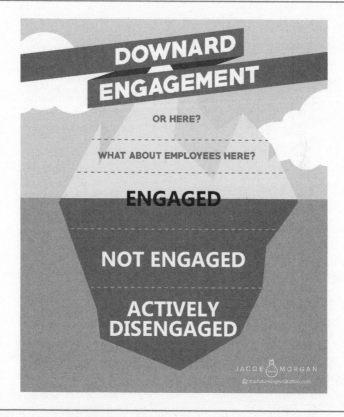

FIGURE 3.1   Employee Engagement Measures Average Employees Who Are Either Below Or Just Above Water, What About the Rest?

C. Hiring for passion and the ability to drive the organization forward is something any business leader looks for and asks about during an interview. If employees don't help move the company forward and they don't feel a connection to the company, then they have no business being there and perhaps we should also ask how they got there to begin with? Organizations bringing in these types of employees must review their hiring practices. I know it's harsh but that doesn't make it any less true.

A not engaged employee is the equivalent of a D, and an actively disengaged employee is a big fat F. So looking at this model, the best that an organization can do is hire an average employee who will perform as expected. Everyone else is either below or very below average. Imagine what kind of an organization this creates, better yet, we know what kinds of organizations this creates as evidenced by the current engagement scores around the world.

What about the employees who do feel a sense of passion and who go above and beyond what is expected of them to help others? Or, what about the super employees who constantly exceed expectations and act as brand cheerleaders even when not at work? These types of employees don't fit into the traditional model of engagement. This is what I mean when I say employee engagement is stuck measuring downward instead of upward. You can be only a C employee or worse when looking at this type of a model.

Engagement Has Become the New Annual Review

Organizations question the value of annual employee reviews yet for some reason are okay with measuring employee engagement every year. This makes no sense. In many cases employee engagement surveys are simply replacing the annual review and are becoming the very thing that organizations are trying to get rid of! There is no right answer for how often you should measure employee engagement. That's something I believe your people should control and be able to do when and where they want as often as they want. Organizations need to understand that this is a dynamic and fluid thing that changes constantly. We are not light switches that are either on or off.

Anything related to people should be measured continuously. Perhaps you have a short single-question pulse survey weekly, monthly culture snapshots, semiannual engagement reviews, and a larger state of the company survey. Of course, this is just an illustrative example to show that doing one annual survey may not give you an accurate reflection of what's going on inside of your company. Some companies I've spoken with don't even look at people metrics annually. They might do so only once every few years! If annual reviews don't do a good job of measuring employee performance, then annual engagement surveys don't make much sense for measuring the pulse of the organization.

Another approach that some organizations, such as General Electric (GE), take is to run constant surveys to random employees. So you might do a survey for 1,000 employees one month, another thousand the following month, and so on. The idea is to get employee data and feedback constantly from a representative sample size of the organization. For an organization like GE that has over 300,000 employees around the world, this approach makes much more sense than trying to do one annual survey. I'll talk about this a bit later in the book as well.

Engagement Tends to Look at the Effect but Not the Cause

In most models the ideal scenario for organizations is to get as many engaged employees as possible. They do this maniacally as if they are collecting Pokémon characters. It's as if for every engaged employee an organization gets, it will level up and will finally be able to take on that giant monster! Unfortunately, many organizations get so stuck focusing on engagement that they forget to take a step back to understand what causes engagement to begin with let alone understand the impact that engaged employees are having on the organization. This means that engagement just boils down to a number, and a number without context is quite useless. If you recall the famous book and movie *The Hitchhiker's Guide to the Galaxy*, the answer to "What's the meaning of life?" is 42. It's just a number as are most employee engagement scores that organizations receive. You scored a 68? Wonderful! A 92? Even better! Now what? Does this mean if you get to 100 you can stop? See what I'm getting at here? The cause is employee experience; the effect is an engaged workforce.

Engagement Surveys Are Exhaustingly Long

It's common for employee engagement surveys to be well over 100 questions long that ask pretty much everything and anything. This makes me think of my college days when I had to take multiple choice tests on scantrons (remember those?). Those exams were around 30 to 40 questions, and sometimes we even got a 15-minute break! Who in his or her right mind would want to sit and take an exam about his or her organization, and more important, who would actually sit through and answer all the questions honestly?! Speaking of honesty, let's not forget that employee engagement surveys can also be manipulated. I once spoke with a chief human resources officer of a global company who told me that if she wanted to increase her employee engagement score quickly, then she would ask employees to take it once on a cloudy, rainy day and then again on a sunny day. Boom! Ten point improvement! Some organizations also have the scary habit of manipulating their engagement scores by either offering incentives to get people to score higher or reprimanding employees who don't score their organizations high enough.

Engagement Acts as an Adrenaline Shot

One of the things that I find quite fascinating is when people start working at an organization, they are already engaged. Rarely have I talked to an employee just starting out at an organization who says, "Man, this job is terrible!" The exact opposite is actually true. When employees start working for an organization, they are typically excited to be there and are very much looking forward to being a part of your team and making an impact. Think back to the jobs you have had in the past. You may have been a bit nervous or scared when starting a new job, but chances are that you rarely started being unhappy or disengaged. So something happens to turn these already engaged and happy employees into unhappy and disengaged people. Right about this time the organization does one of its employee engagement surveys, and when it sees the negative results, managers say, "What? Our engagement scores are that low? Quick, we need to do something!" At that point some new perks might be introduced. Maybe a flexible work approach is implemented, some office layout changes might happen, and perhaps catered meals a few times a week are introduced because clearly free food makes us happier. Then things improve a bit on the engagement score temporarily before dropping off again and the same cycle repeats itself as you can see in figure 3.2. Basically engagement in many organizations acts as an adrenaline shot to temporarily boost employee happiness and satisfaction whereas employee experience is the ongoing design of the organization. Unfortunately engagement efforts simply feel like manipulation and thus doesn't create trust or loyalty and does nothing to unlock human potential which also means no business impact for the organization.

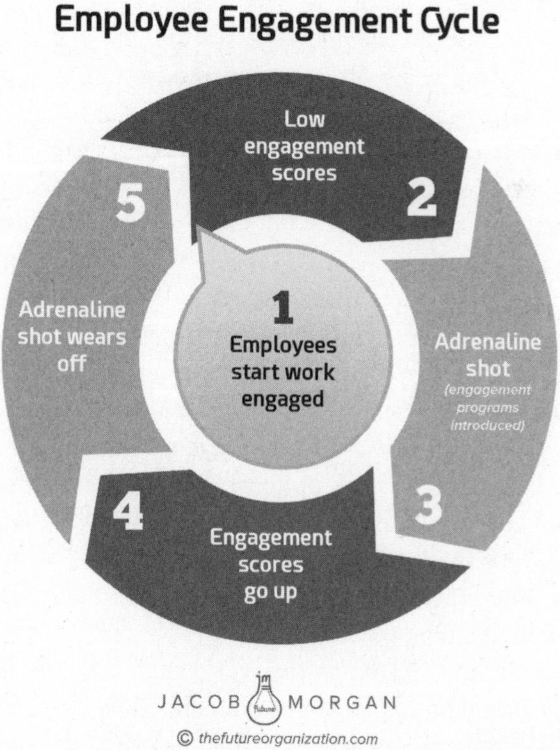

Employee Engagement Cycle

JACOB MORGAN
© thefutureorganization.com

FIGURE 3.2   Employee Engagement as the Short-Term Adrenaline Shot Instead of the Long-Term (Re)design of the Organization

Employee engagement has been a wonderful tool for us to think differently about our organizations, but it's also been used as a bit of a crutch to justify the existence and importance of human resources (HR) as a function. We also have to remember that just because you measure something doesn't mean you improve it. While there's nothing wrong with continuing to measure employee engagement, it's time for us to look at a new approach for a rapidly changing world that is focused on the long-term designing of employee experiences which then yields an engaged workforce.

In fact, I believe that employee engagement can and should simply be measured by asking employees one question. What that question is can certainly vary from one organization to the next. When doing research for this book, I wanted to say it should be something along the lines of "Do you wake up every morning wanting to go to work?" Although this type of a question is tempting to ask, I don't think it's the right approach. In other words how an employee feels is not a good indicator of engagement, but what he or she actually does is. This is why I think a question such as "Do you show up to work every day with the intention of helping others succeed?" is far better suited to measure engagement. Success in this case is a very subjective metric that can mean anything from helping people feel good to actually helping them deliver on a project, but in this case the subjectivity is a good thing. When I spoke with Pat Wadors, the CHRO at LinkedIn, she told me that if she could pick just one way to measure engagement at her company, it would be "If employees show up to work each day wanting to create a sense of belonging for others." In Pat's case she has the data to back up the significant positive correlation between this criterion and employee engagement. Focusing on an action is better than focusing on a feeling because it looks at a tangible impact.

Beth Taska is the CHRO of the world's largest gym, 24 Hour Fitness. When I met with her in 2016, she echoed what Pat told me. The whole point of employee engagement is to unlock the discretionary effort within employees. This is the amount of effort that employees could put in if they actually wanted to. But what does that mean? If you think about most of the interactions you have daily with various brands, you will realize that they are very linear and static. There is very little differ-entiation. Whether you go to a retail store, a supermarket to purchase groceries, a check-in gate to board a flight, or a restaurant to order food, you pretty much know what will happen and what to expect. It's always the same thing. So how is it that some organizations are able to go above and beyond to deliver customer experiences? The answer is discretionary effort. What organizations like LinkedIn and 24 Hour Fitness have fig-ured out is that when you focus on employee experiences, employees go above and beyond to help not only one another but also your customers. Discretionary effort is measured in terms of an action, which is why I believe that measuring something like "if employees help others become more successful" is more meaningful and telling than simply asking, "Do you feel a connection to the organization?"

At organizations like wireless provider T-Mobile, this level of discretionary effort all comes down to the impact that employees have on their customers. I spoke with Marty Pisciotti, T-Mobile's vice president of employee careers, who told me that across T-Mobile in the United States, every employee knows the first line of the company values, "Frontline first, because customers are first." T-Mobile believes that frontline employees always come first because the better they are treated, the better they will treat their customers. T-Mobile realized that when employees feel like the company cares, they start to act more like owners who are empowered to truly go above and beyond a traditional job description. To further get this point across, the company introduced a program over three years ago that gives all employees—including those in retail and customer care call centers—stock in the company, which is vested over a three-year period. These are free shares in the company that T-Mobile gives to all employees to help them feel like they are truly making an impact on the business, are vested in the success of the organization, and are able to unlock their maximum potential.

While employee experience needs to look at many aspects of the organization and requires several questions to determine and measure, employee engagement needs just one. So what's the one question you could ask your employees to determine whether they are indeed engaged? Go ask it.

THE WAR FOR TALENT

When you hear the phrase *the war for talent*, it should make you wonder, "When have we ever not been in a war for talent?" Ever since the dawn of modern business, organizations have been seeking to attract and retain the best possible people they could. This isn't new. *The war for talent* is actually a phrase coined in 1997 by Steven Hankin of McKinsey & Company that is meant to refer to the changing landscape around attracting and retaining talent, basically, that it's getting more challenging. This was 30 years ago. Today it's not just challenging. It's downright hard and complex. In a report called *War for Talent—Time to Change Direction*, KPMG surveyed HR professionals around the world, and 59 percent reported that "There is a new war for talent and this time it is different than in the past."[3]

Facebook understands this better than most. It starts with one simple question, which is "If you had the best talent in the world, what would you need to do to attract and retain them?" Organizations like Facebook aren't just looking for people; they are also looking for the best people. This is perhaps one of the largest changes we are starting to see. Technology is replacing bodies, which means that organizations are looking for something more We also have to remember that the war for talent isn't just about attracting potential employees but also keeping existing ones.

Let's break the war for talent down a bit further. The war for talent is being fueled by a few things.

Skills Gap and Talent Shortage

A *McKinsey Quarterly* article by Richard Dobbs, Susan Lund, and Anu Madgavkar titled "Talent Tensions Ahead: A CEO Briefing" stated that "new research from the McKinsey Global Institute (MGI) suggests that by 2020, the world could have 40 million too few college-educated workers and that developing economies may face a shortfall of 45 million workers with secondary-school educations and vocational training. In advanced economies, up to 95 million workers could lack the skills needed for employment."[4] The most recent ManpowerGroup Talent

Shortage Survey of "more than 41,000 hiring managers in 42 countries and territories found that 38% of employers are having difficulty filling jobs."[5] There is little agreement on what is causing this skills gap, what the potential solutions are, and whether the skills gap is even a real thing! Most of the executives I speak with acknowledge that the skills gap is real. Perhaps what makes this even more challenging is that we aren't sure what the jobs of the future will be or when they will be here. Consider that by the time most people graduate from college, the skills and the things they have learned are mostly rendered obsolete. This means organizations are looking to hire employees for jobs that don't yet exist. Not only do we have a skills gap, but we also have a skills uncertainty. The number one thing that potential and current employees can do to succeed in this type of environment is to learn how to learn. In other words, have the ability to learn new things regularly and apply the things that you learn to new and current situations and scenarios. This is further evidenced by the dozens of publicly available conversations I have had with CHROs at the world's largest companies. You can listen to and read about all of these discussions by visiting https://thefutureorganization.com/future-work-podcast/.

What's fascinating is that organizations that focus on creating employee experiences aren't feeling this skills gap as much as those who aren't. It appears that in the coming years, organizations are going to want to hire people, and there just won't be enough high-skilled labor to go around.

Changing Demographics

According to a report by Robert I. Lerman and Stefanie R. Schmidt called *An Overview of Economic, Social, and Demographic Trends Affecting the US Labor Market*:

> BLS [Bureau of Labor Statistics] projections imply that over the next decade, 40 million people will enter the workforce, about 25 million will leave the workforce, and 109 million will remain. Although only a modest reduction will take place in the overall

growth in the workforce (from 1.3 percent per year to 1.1 percent per year), the composition of growth will generate rising shares of young (under 25) and older (45 and over) workers and a decline in the share of middle-age workers.[6]

We are already starting to see this trend. Today, millennials are already the largest demographic, surpassing baby boomers in 2016. By 2020 they are expected to comprise 50 percent of the workforce, and by 2025 this is expected to be 75 percent of the workforce. We also see Gen Z (the generation after the millennials) creeping into the workplace as well, and they currently comprise over 25 million people in the United States alone. Not only that but also the labor participation rate in the United States appears to be gradually yet consistently shrinking. This changing mix of demographics brings new values, attitudes, expectations, and ways of working. Still, this isn't new. Our organizations have always had to adapt to new generations entering the workforce, but the overall sense is that previous adaptations were very slow and gradual and have now become more aggressive.

Changing Face of Talent Competition

In the past organizations used to compete on a few levels, which were typically skills and seniority, location, and direct rivals. This meant that if you lived in San Francisco, you would compete against other people in the area, or that if you were Coca-Cola, you'd compete against Pepsi, Ford versus Toyota, Boeing versus Airbus, or McDonald's versus Burger King. Today, with the exception of certain specialized skills and roles, everyone is competing with everyone. Coca-Cola is competing against Toyota and McDonald's is competing against Airbus. Not only that but organizations are also competing on a global scale (read globalization) in a world where many perceive a skills shortage in an environment that is seeing traditional employment and business models change. This competition also extends to the gig economy, where smart and talented individuals might decide to drive for Uber or join an online freelance marketplace instead of working for you.

Psychology (and Sociology)

Employee experience is very much a psychological and sociological pursuit as many of the concepts around team building, motivation, performance, and success are influenced by studies that psychologists and sociologists have been conducting for decades (there are several referenced in this book). Any business book that you pick up today is bound to have several mentions of this. Organizations are now taking these pursuits more seriously as they try to truly create environments where people want to show up to work. This is no longer just a challenge that an organization can overcome with perks, higher pay, or gimmicks. Instead the business world is turning to the social scientists to really help them understand why and how people tick. It should come as no surprise that according to the U.S. Bureau of Labor Statistics, industrial organizational psychology is one of the fastest growing professions. These scientists are influencing how we hire and recruit people, design our office spaces, lead and manage, and even build and run our HR departments. Organizations such as Johnson & Johnson work with teams of psychologists for these exact purposes. This too speaks to the trend toward focusing on longer-term organizational design instead of shorter-term engagement programs.

Business Turbulence

According to Mark J. Perry of the American Enterprise Institute, a public policy think tank, almost 90 percent of the Fortune 500 have disappeared since the original list was created in 1955.[7] In the past to really disrupt a large global company, you had to be a large global company. Not only that but also these organizations usually had a sense of where their threats were coming from. Today competition can come from a door-to-door fax salesperson (Spanx), a college dropout (Facebook), a former customer (Netflix), or someone who just raises a ton of money (Uber and Airbnb). The point is that in a world that appears to be getting smaller, at a time when change is getting faster, your competition can come from anywhere, and you'll never see it until it's in your face. In this environment organizations are struggling to hire the best talent that will help them see potential threats and uncover new opportunities. By focusing on employee experience many companies are hoping to be able to reverse that trend.

TECHNOLOGY

The proliferation of mobile devices with global connectivity allows us to work anywhere and anytime. Videoconferencing and internal social networks allow us to communicate and collaborate at scale without any boundaries. On-demand platforms, such as Catalant, Upwork, and Kaggle, allow organizations to quickly scale their workforce up or down while being able to access top talent anywhere in the world. Big data (and its analysis) is allowing us to gain new insight into how we work, why we work, and what we can do to drive performance, experience, and engagement. Robots and automation are predicted to replace many jobs around the world, leaving a questionable future of employment. This is why I was so shocked to see the lack of discussion and debate around automation and job displacement during the recent presidential election. We are worried about losing jobs to other countries but it appears that the larger threat may be losing jobs inside of our country to software and AI. This is why the discussions around Universal Basic Income are becoming so prevalent. The idea is that if AI and automation replace many people around the world, that giving everyone a guaranteed regular income can solve the financial burden of not having a job. UBI is a widely contested topic that still has many questions which need to be answered.

The Internet of things promises to create a connected world which along with artificial intelligence will yield more productivity, efficiency, and abundance. Virtual and augmented reality will change the way we interact with physical and virtual worlds by combining and overlaying the two. The list goes on and on.

Technology is not only enabling us to work more effectively, but it's also creating entirely new ways of working in addition to creating new jobs and eliminating many older ones. What I find fascinating is that in the past, progressive views around how work can and should be done were stalled by not having technologies to actually enable those new ways of working. Today organizations have access to technologies that can enable and empower almost anything that can be thought of. Technology has caught up to and has indeed far surpassed what our organizations can actually implement. The sky's the limit!

I give around 40 keynote talks around the world each year. Regardless of the audience or the location I speak at, technology is consistently ranked as the top (or one of the top) thing that attendees believe will affect their organizations. Later in the book I'll explore the role of technology and automation on employee experience, but a full look at how technology is affecting the future of work is beyond the scope of this book. If you want to learn more, there are several great resources on this very topic, including a free, 150-page report the University of Oxford and Citi published called *Technology at Work v2.0*.

We must also remember that technology is but one aspect in a changing world. Before various technologies can be scaled and adopted there are many other things which must be considered. Futurists use a framework with the acronym STEEPLE which stands for: Social, Technological, Economic, Environmental, Political, Legal, and Ethical. Notice that technology is just one of the seven things which need to be looked at. Take the autonomous vehicle as an example. There is little doubt that the technology is there today to produce a fully functioning self-driving car. But how long will it take for us to see this at scale and how long before these vehicles will displace all of the human drivers today? We need to consider things such as insurance, infrastructure, rules and regulations, ownership, security, production, and much more before we can see these cars take over. Today the autonomous cars you see actually have two drivers instead of one. One driver sits in the driver seat as a backup and another sits in the passenger seat and collects data. We haven't even touched on the comfort level of people getting into an autonomous vehicle or the ethical challenges that we need to explore. For example, how does a self-driving car decide between an unavoidable accident where it will either risk the life of the passenger or risk the life of a bystander?

Technology is indeed a powerful disruptor but it must be placed in context of what else is required for that technology to scale and have an impact.

ALTERNATIVE WORK ARRANGEMENTS AND THE GIG ECONOMY

Does focusing on employee experience even make sense in a world that is supposedly going to be dominated by freelancers and short-term employees? There's been a lot of debate and confusion around this space, so it only makes sense to explore what's going on here. The umbrella term that nontraditional employment models fall under is *alternative work arrangements*. This includes everyone from Uber drivers to construction workers who work on independent contracts to those of us who work with staffing agencies for temporary employment. Figure 3.3 should help clarify what all of this looks like. When most people refer to the gig or freelance economy, they are specifically referring to people who work through online intermediary sites, such as Uber, Upwork, and Airbnb.

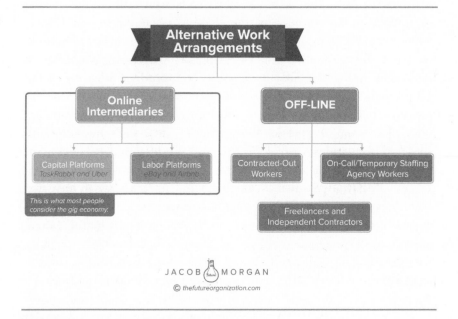

FIGURE 3.3   Alternative Work Arrangements

Source: Lawrence F. Katz and Alan B. Krueger.[8]

To make things easier we will refer to this as the *online gig economy* for the rest of this section. You will see where that term came from later. With that context in mind we can look at what's going on. The image in Figure 3.3 shows the broader category of alternative work and where the online platforms fit in.

Growing Fast but Not Dominating

The first thing we need to understand is that although the online gig economy is growing, it is by no means going to dominate the workforce, not even close. The vast majority of us will continue to be full-time employees the way we are today. It's true our workforce will be more dynamic and fluid, but employment as we know it won't be going anywhere.

Ted Egan is the chief economist for the Office of the Controller in the City and County of San Francisco. Recently he released a report called *The Gig Economy in San Francisco: Prevalence, Growth, and Implications*. In it he cited the JPMorgan Chase Institute, which found that as of September 2015 in the United States, the "percentage of adults who earned income from online platforms" (such as Uber, Upwork, Airbnb, and the like) in the past year was just over 3 percent, and this isn't even people who make a full-time living from freelancing (that number is undoubtedly much smaller). Even in San Francisco, the supposed home for innovation and technology, wage employment has still been growing faster than self-employment.[9]

In a 2016 article by Emily Green for *SFGate* called "Gig Work Isn't Changing Job Landscape, SF Economist Finds," Robert Habans, a research associate at the University of California, Los Angeles, Institute for Research on Labor and Employment, summed up this fascination with the gig economy (again specifically looking at online intermediaries) wonderfully. He said, "It's kind of hard to reconcile that [findings from Egan's report] with how intensely everybody is talking about the gig economy, especially in a place like San Francisco. Most recent studies have failed to demonstrate a wholesale shift toward the gig economy, including this one." In that same article Lawrence Mishel, from the

Economic Policy Institute (and someone whom I had the privilege of discussing this at length with), said, "Digital platform work is just a small part of a broader set of employment practices."[10]

Another fascinating paper by Seth D. Harris, the former U.S. secretary of labor and now professor at Cornell University, and Alan B. Krueger, an economist at Princeton University and former chairman on the White House Council of Economic Advisers, called *A Proposal for Modernizing Labor Laws for Twenty-First-Century Work: The "Independent Worker* found that "about 600,000 workers, or 0.4 percent of total U.S. employment, work with an online intermediary in the gig economy," such as Uber or TaskRabbit.[11]

Lawrence F. Katz, a professor of economics at Harvard, and Alan B. Krueger, published a fantastic presentation called "The Rise of Alternative Work Arrangements & the 'Gig' Economy." The term they used to refer to online intermediaries is the *online gig economy*, which is what I have used here.

Although they have found the online gig economy to be quite tiny, they also found that it is growing remarkably quickly. In fact they cited Diana Farrell and Fiona Greig's 2016 finding that there was a 10× increase in the percentage of adults participating in the online gig economy each month and a 47× increase in the cumulative percentage of adults who have ever participated in the online gig economy. These are truly remarkable numbers. Another interesting but perhaps not surprising finding from the presentation is that Uber could represent half to two-thirds of all online gig economy work. If you were to remove Uber from the equation, the online gig economy would be almost nonexistent.

However, if we look at the broader category of alternative work arrangements, we appear to see a very different story, one of much larger growth and impact. According to same presentation by Katz and Krueger, "All net U.S. employment growth since 2005 appears to be in alternative work arrangements." This category has grown from 10.1 percent of all employment in February 2005 to an estimate of 15.8 percent at the end of 2015, or around 24 million people, based on Katz and Krueger's analysis of their 2015 survey Bureau of Labor Statistics data.[12]

Another piece of evidence I'll mention here is a great article published by Josh Zumbrun and Anna Louie Sussman in the *Wall Street Journal* called "Proof of a 'Gig Economy' Revolution Is Hard to Find." According to the article, "Official government data shows around 95% of those who report having jobs are accounted for on the formal payroll of U.S. employers, little changed from a decade ago." The article continues, "But the share of people who hold multiple jobs is also in decline—only 4.8% of workers do, down from 5.5% in 2005 and 6.3% in 1995."[13]

These are a few of the many studies that have been done that show that the gig economy as we know it (looking at online intermediaries) is tiny (but growing). The studies I mention here have been conducted with academic rigor and are among the best efforts I have seen undertaken to quantify the true size of the gig economy. I want to stress the importance here of the academic rigor because there are plenty of other studies that have the size of the gig economy exponentially larger. These studies are oftentimes done by organizations that have a vested interest in inflating numbers and they do so by asking questions guaranteed to do so. For example they might ask if in the past 12 months you have done some form of work for money, which falls outside the realm of a traditional job, if you answer "yes" then oftentimes you are labeled as a freelancer. There are all sorts of things that I might do once a year like go sky diving, scuba diving, try a new food, and the like. But I don't tell people I'm a sky or scuba diver!

The Effect on Employee Tenure

Another popular theory that has been circulating is that employee tenure is in rapid decline and that in the near future we will all be portfolio employees where instead of working for a single employer, we will work for many employers at the same time. As someone who has made a living based on portfolio model [I work with over 40 companies a year], I'd be happy to see this become reality, but again, the data doesn't seem to support this direction.

According to the U.S. Census Bureau data Craig Copeland cited, "Data show that the overall median tenure of workers—the midpoint of

wage and salary workers' length of employment in their current jobs—
was slightly higher in 2014, at 5.5 years, compared with 5.0 years in
1983."[14] Granted the report is three years old, but it's the most current one as of this writing. I find this quite interesting because from all
the executives whom I speak with, there is a consensus that employee
tenure is not what it used to be and is in fact shrinking. It's hard to look
at national averages and then apply those averages to specific companies. As you can imagine if you are in a hot labor market, such as San
Francisco or New York, the tenure might be different than if you're
in a part of the country like Wyoming or Minnesota. The industry also
has a dramatic impact. Those in the technology industry won't have the
same tenure as those in the construction industry. Although the data
shows that tenure seems to be growing, many of the executives I speak
with would disagree and dispute these numbers as they relate to their
respective organizations.

This isn't just an American thing either. According to the Chartered
Institute of Personnel and Development in the United Kingdom, which
published a report called "Megatrends: The Trends Shaping Work and
Working Lives":

> While self-employment has increased in the last 30 years, some
> four-fifths of people working in the UK are still permanent
> employees. In addition, the average period of time people spend
> with an employer did not shift greatly between the mid-1970s
> and the mid-2000s, albeit with some changes within the overall
> average. Furthermore, our evidence suggests that job turnover
> in the UK has been falling over the past decade—meaning that
> fewer people change employers each year.[15]

Are all of these reports perfect and all the numbers 100 percent
accurate? Absolutely not. It's hard for anyone to provide accurate
numbers around how large the alternate work category is, especially the
online gig economy portion of that. That's because the U.S. government
stopped collecting any data on the contingent workforce many years ago.
However, early in 2016 Tom Perez, the U.S. secretary of labor,

announced that the government will once again start tracking this data as a part of the 2017 population survey. This is very exciting because we will finally get some accurate numbers around how big this space really is.

Does this mean we don't need to pay attention to the gig economy or alternative work arrangements? Of course not. Instead of just looking at total numbers today, it's also helpful for us to look at where things might be going. The numbers can sometimes appear to be conflicting, but based on all the research and data that exist, it's safe to say that today the gig economy as it pertains to online platforms is a very tiny fraction of the workforce. Alternative work arrangements in general (including the gig economy) are growing and adoption rates are staggeringly high. However, today many people are using these platforms as ways to augment existing work arrangements and income. This forces us to ask a broader economical question, "Why is it that so many people feel the need to augment their existing incomes, and if we paid them more, would they continue to do so?"

Data also shows that employee tenure isn't shrinking as rapidly as previously thought. It may actually be increasing but slightly. It's important to keep in mind that this is simply an average. Although I have personally heard of many accounts of decreasing employee tenure from various executives at global organizations, they don't represent the average. This is yet another reason why people analytics has to be leveraged so that each organization can understand its own truths. As Wayne Gretzky famously said, "I skate to where the puck is going to be, not where it has been." While we are still in the relatively early stages of alternative work and the gig economy, organizations should absolutely stay aware of the changes that are happening in this space.

This should be enough information to get you to think again when you hear someone talking about the end of employment as we know it. This should also help you understand why employee experience is so crucial, because full-time employment isn't going away in the near future. So the long answer to "Does focusing on employee experience even make sense in a world that is supposedly going to be dominated by freelancers and short-term employees?" is a resounding yes.

PEOPLE ANALYTICS

This is a core foundation for being able to create employee experiences. Ranjan Dutta is the director of people analytics at Pricewaterhouse-Coopers (PwC), and he leads a team of hundreds of leaders who work with organizations around the world on their people analytics strategies. When we spoke he told me that organizations have three things that essentially make up their business: money, material, and people. In today's world any company can replicate your business model, the goods you produce, or the services you offer. The one thing that organizations cannot copy is your people. People are your greatest competitive advantage. So how do organizations get the very best out of their people? This is what people analytics helps organizations do. It gives organizations the data and the insight they need to make people-related decisions. People analytics also empowers organizations to test ideas and run experiments.

According to Ranjan marketing has gone through this very evolution. If you recall, decades ago marketing wasn't very data driven. It was based on ideas and intuition and was very touchy-feely. Today marketing is based on all sorts of data. Organizations are doing customer segmentation, journey mapping, doing competitor analysis, and measuring and testing every aspect of how people interact with brands and their products. Amazon tests its home page many times a day. In fact, the home page I see will be different from the home page you see. Amazon uses data to make decisions around what content their visitors should see. What if we could apply a similar concept inside of organizations?

The concept of scientific management was based on the idea of using metrics and measurement to improve how employees work. Employees were literally timed with stopwatches to shave seconds off their tasks. We've come a long way since then, and today HR organizations (and others) around the world are staffing up with data scientists and analysts to help them make sense of all the data they have on their employees (big data) and to figure out what other data can be collected. This is quite a new and emerging area of practice. Many large organizations I have spoken with have yet to build advanced capabilities around it, but they are all planning to. Organizations today have lots of data about their employees, including salary, tenure, satisfaction, ratings and reviews, performance, and much more. The trouble is that few organizations have a way of putting all of this information together to understand their employees.

The data is actually quite diverse and combines everything from organizational data (such as looking at an organizational chart or revenue) to individual data (such as compensation and tenure) to emotional or psychological data (such as engagement and job satisfaction). But what about other external data that an employee provides as well? On a resume you can look at where employees went to school, what they majored in, what their GPA was, what extracurricular activities they participated in, what awards they won, whom they are connected to, and so on. I believe resumes are on their way out and are being replaced by sites such as LinkedIn, which make it easy to get all sorts of data about a prospective candidate or a current employee. As you can see, the data sources are diverse, and the amount of data is vast.

In 2016 I traveled to Zürich, Switzerland, to meet with a large financial institution. During a discussion with its executive leaders, they shared two interesting facts with me. The first was that people tend to stay at this company for a long time, and the second was that when people do leave the company, it usually happens at around the two-year mark. My two questions were then "Why do people stay at the company for a long time?" and "What is it about the two-year mark that causes employees to leave?" The organization didn't know either. Granted it is in the process of building up a people analytics team to be able to answer exactly these types of questions. For a long time we also assumed that people who go to top-tier universities and get high GPAs will also perform better inside of our organizations. Well, people analytics has now helped us realize that where you went to school and how well you did in school don't predict how well you will do at work.

What if you knew:

- What qualities make a great manager
- When employees get burned out
- What makes employees most productive

- Why employees leave or stay
- How to get teams to collaborate across teams and geographies
- How to get employees to be healthier
- How activities outside of work affect employees at work

This is just a smidgeon of what people analytics can help you figure out. If you notice, these aren't just HR challenges. These are also business challenges that affect every team across the company, from sales and marketing to manufacturing, research and development, HR, and customer service. Essentially every organization is going to become its own research firm that will be able to ask and answer any questions that arise. Prasad Setty is the vice president, people analytics and compensation, at Google, and he has a saying: "All people decisions at Google are based on data and analytics."

People Analytics in Action

Anshul Sheopuri is the director of the people analytics team at IBM, which now comprises over 70 employees and started around 2010, so these guys have been doing this for seven years already and are considered veterans in the people analytics game. Thanks to this team, IBM has been able to reduce employee churn by 2 percent by using data analytics to enable managers to deliver personalized coaching and guidance to employees. They also launched something called Blue Matching, which was designed to improve internal mobility inside of the company, as opposed to employees looking for opportunities outside of the company. Using analytics, employees get personalized job alerts based on their skills, performance, location, and area of expertise. To date over 40,000 employees have participated, and almost 500 job placements have been made. These are 500 potential employees who would have left IBM to go elsewhere.

Microsoft also saw an issue with internal mobility and because of people analytics was able to make policy changes that made it easier for employees to move around inside of the company instead of going elsewhere. Using various data points, such as compensation, tenure, and job performance, LinkedIn is able to create a type of heat map that helps managers better determine when an employee might be a potential flight risk, that is, he or she is getting ready or wants to leave the organization to look for other opportunities. This allows LinkedIn to intervene before that happens.

PwC wanted to test out the value of people analytics internally, so it asked Ranjan and his team (composed of 25 people analytics practitioners who focus internally at PwC) for a kind of test project. Like LinkedIn, PwC wanted to see if they could predict which employees would leave the company at around the 12-month mark. Sure enough right around that time, the company started to notice that the people Ranjan and his team identified as going to leave actually started leaving. PwC also had a big assumption around recruiting from Ivy League schools. It believed that employees who were recruited from the top-tier universities would perform better than everyone else. Thanks to people analytics, this was proved false. In fact employees who were recruited from non–Ivy League schools performed better than those who were. This allowed PwC to redistribute its recruiting funds and focus on different universities.

Ashley Goodall is the senior vice president of leadership and team intelligence at Cisco, and when I spoke with him he made a great point that too many organizations get stuck using people analytics to compute averages instead of focusing on what he believes to be far more important, excellence. In other words it's far more useful to understand something such as what the best leaders do and how the best teams work instead of how leaders and teams work on average. This concept of averages is what many organizations around the world then use to assign people an annual performance ranking, which Cisco has since gotten rid of. Cisco actually also got rid of its annual employee engagement survey as well. By the time it would launch the survey and then analyze it, slice and dice it by function, share it, develop a plan around it, and actually implement it, at least five months would go by. At that point the managers would respond to the information and say something like "Great, thanks for the plan but unfortunately four people are no longer on the team, we have shifted gears to focus on a new project, and half the team now works from home." The problem with most people analytics efforts is that they provide data that is too broad, to people who can't do anything with it, at a period when no action can be taken. To solve this problem Cisco has shifted its approach to focus on experience and engagement at the team level. I should also point out that at Cisco many employees are a part of more than one team, working across functions and regions. In fact, when Ashley and his team were doing their research, they found that over 25 percent of the teams at Cisco were unaccounted for, meaning they didn't know these teams even existed because they weren't on the organizational chart!

Today, any team leader at Cisco can run an eight-question pulse survey anytime he or she wants to get an idea of what's going on in the team. These responses are then analyzed and reported back in a matter of two to six days instead of six months. Then, the analysis is customized based on what the leader's strengths are and provides strategies around how to improve. From these eight questions Cisco can look at team information and organizational information (by aggregating individual team–based information). Ashley admitted that Cisco doesn't have all the answers, but they are learning and adapting as they go, always with the aim of empowering teams to become better.

Organizations must do their own internal research to find out their own truth. What I mean by that is it's easy for us to read research reports and studies from analyst and consulting firms and then assume that what we read applies to us. If a study says millennials are job-hopping, then it means our millennials are job hoppers. If a study says diversity is an issue, then diversity must be an issue for us. If a research report says engagement is at an all-time low, then our engagement must be at an all-time low. None of these conclusions make sense. Although looking at external research can provide some broader context around certain things, the information should all be taken with a grain of salt. If you truly want answers to questions and if you truly want to know what the research says, then conduct your own inside of your organization. That's the only way to make business decisions, especially those that pertain to your people.

The Future of People Analytics

According to Ben Waber, the founder and CEO of Humanyze, this is all just the tip of the iceberg. I first met Ben in Madrid, where we were both speaking at a conference. Ben got his PhD at Massachusetts Institute of Technology in the Human Dynamics group and has studied behavioral analytics for many years. His company creates badges (just like employee ID badges) that employees wear at work. Except these badges are different. They are equipped with a variety of sensors, such as radio-frequency ID that allow the badges to act like true ID badges, Bluetooth that measures someone's location in an office, infrared that can tell who you are facing, and a microphone that measures not what you say, but how you say it and how much time you spend speaking. These are things that actually measure human behavior, which according to Ben is something that most organizations don't measure.

This type of data can be used to help organizations understand things such as whether marketing is talking to engineering, whether the manager of a team actually spends time with his or her people, what the top-performing employees in certain roles do differently, and how the most successful salespeople speak with their customers. Although organizations oftentimes do A/B testing for customer-facing initiatives, this type of approach is rarely done inside of organizations simply because the behavioral data doesn't exist, but eventually it will. This will allow organizations to optimize and improve everything from how teams are structured to how compensation packages are created. Imagine being able to A/B test how work gets done regularly. Ben acknowledges that survey data is still useful and important to have, but it paints only a part of the picture. In the next decade or so, only a handful of companies will get to this level of behavior analytics.

In most organizations I have observed, the people analytics function sits in HR or sometimes it's a separate function. This makes perfect sense because HR typically deals with people. The challenge today is that many HR teams don't have this capability because it's a new skill set. HR has primarily always been about dealing with people and their interactions, legal, hiring, and firing versus actually analyzing people from a data science perspective. However, as this area becomes more advanced, it is quite possible that it will grow into its own department that reports directly to the CEO.

There is, of course, a dark side to people analytics because data can be used to make decisions that either positively affect people or negatively affect people. For example, people analytics can be used for calculating mass layoffs or for determining ways to manipulate people. This is a delicate balance that organizations have to be careful of, not to mention the potential creepy factor of employees having data collected about their every move and action! Not only that but people analytics models are designed by people which means they will be inherently flawed. In her wonderful book, *Weapons of Math Destruction*, Cathy O'Neil tells the story of a middle-school teacher named Sarah Wysocki who was let go from a job with the Washington DC school district because an algorithm decided that she was doing a poor job. The school district was determined to improve underperforming schools by eliminating bad teachers. Although she got rave reviews from the principal and from parents, somehow she was classified as being in the bottom 2% of teachers. It turns out the elementary school where Susan's students came from was one of several schools under investigation for a high likelihood of cheating on standardized tests by teachers who were erasing the wrong answers and filling in the correct ones. They did this to help preserve their own jobs. This meant that when Susan's students took standardized tests where no cheating was involved, their scores dropped considerably, thus making it look like they weren't getting the education they should have been. Naturally the teacher was to blame. In this situation the algorithm would have no way of picking this up and as a result Susan and over 200 other teachers were fired. This story illustrates just how important it is for us to not place all of our decision-making eggs in the people analytics basket.

Today we are still at the very early stages of what's possible. Perhaps the biggest challenge for companies today is organizing, cleaning, aggregating, and standardizing data, a project that can easily take years, depending on the size of the organization.

With technology advances and the integration of AI, you will one day be able to use voice commands to ask a smart assistant (think Siri, Cortana, Watson, Viv, or Echo) things like:

- "What's the employee turnover?"
- "Who are the top three employees on my team at risk for leaving the organization?"
- "How many contingent workers are we using, and how much are we paying them each year?"
- "What are the top skills and weaknesses on my team?"
- "Which teams are the highest performing inside of our organization?"
- "I need to build a new marketing team in California composed of five individuals; which employees should I consider?"

People analytics is absolutely growing into a core business capability that every organization must invest in heavily and it's the foundation of employee experience

TRANSPARENCY

If you were to rewind the clock 10 to 15 years ago and you worked for an organization that wasn't really treating people well, what could you do? There really wasn't much transparency in the workplace, and employees didn't have much of a voice. This meant that most organizations could pretty much treat employees however they wanted. These organizations had cash and they had brand power, which translated to being able to attract the best talent. Brand power today ain't what it used to be. You don't automatically want to work for a company like Starbucks, Disney, or Ford, just because of the name. These organizations are having to try much harder to get the people they need and want.

Today's world is very different. Not only do we see enormous business turbulence, competition, and pace of change, but also employees today have a voice that they've never had before. Man are they using it! Hundreds of sites around the world rank organizations on everything from being a best place to work to being a diverse organization to offering great flexibility to having an environment with the least amount of stress and everything in between. Combine this with social media sites and transparent career sites like Glassdoor, and you're living in a whole other business world. Organizations cannot afford not to invest in employee experience if even for this one reason. People can and will know everything about your organization even before speaking with anyone who works there. This includes salary information, benefits packages, what your corporate culture is like, questions asked during the interview process, and everything and anything in between. When most people go shopping at a big-box retailer, they usually already know what they want and how much they should pay for it. That's because they have already done the research and know exactly what they want. This same logic applies to the world of people and organizations. If you invest in employee experience, then it pays off in spades because your organization will quickly become known as an amazing place to work. This is something that organizations such as Google, Facebook, Riot Games, and World Wide Technology have figured out rather quickly.

Together, these powerful drivers are forcing organizations to create places where employees genuinely want to show up to work, where employees are able to bring their ideas, their dreams, their aspirations, their hopes, and even their fears to work. We all deserve to work for this type of organization, and the vast majority of employees around the world don't. It's time to fix that.

NOTES

1. Mann, Annamarie, and Jim Harter. "The Worldwide Employee Engagement Crisis." Gallup. January 7, 2016. http://www.gallup.com/businessjournal/188033/worldwide-employee-engagement-crisis.aspx.
2. Aon. *2016 Trends in Global Employee Engagement*. 2016. www.aon.com/ecuador/attachments/Engagement2016.pdf.
3. KPMG International. *War for Talent—Time to Change Direction*. June 2014. https://home.kpmg.com/content/dam/kpmg/pdf/2014/07/war-for-talent.pdf.
4. Dobbs, Richard, Susan Lund, and Anu Madgavkar. "Talent Tensions Ahead: A CEO Briefing." *McKinsey Quarterly*, November 2012. http://www.mckinsey.com/global-themes/employment-and-growth/talent-tensions-ahead-a-ceo-briefing.

5. ManPower Group. "2015 Talent Shortage Results." 2015. http://www.manpower group.com/talent-shortage-2015.

6. Lerman, Robert I., and Stefanie R. Schmidt. *An Overview of Economic, Social, and Demographic Trends Affecting the US Labor Market*. The Urban Institute. February 1999. https://www.dol.gov/dol/aboutdol/history/herman/reports/futurework/conference/trends/trends_toc.htm.

7. Perry, Mark J. "Fortune 500 Firms 1955 v. 2016: Only 12% Remain, Thanks to the Creative Destruction That Fuels Economic Prosperity." *AEIdeas* (blog), December 13, 2016. https://www.aei.org/publication/fortune-500-firms-1955-v-2016-only-12-remain-thanks-to-the-creative-destruction-that-fuels-economic-prosperity/.

8. Katz, Lawrence F., and Alan B. Krueger. "The Rise and Nature of Alternative Work Arrangements in the United States, 1995–2015." National Bureau of Economic Research. September 2016. http://www.nber.org/papers/w22667.

9. Egan, Ted. *The Gig Economy in San Francisco: Prevalence, Growth, and Implications*. Office of the Controller Office of Economic Analysis. July 5, 2016. sfcontroller .org/sites/default/files/Gig%20Economy.final_.pdf.

10. Green, Emily. "Gig Work Isn't Changing Job Landscape, SF Economist Finds." *SFGate*, July 5, 2016. http://www.sfgate.com/bayarea/article/Gig-work-isn-t-changing-job-landscape-SF-8340347.php.

11. Harris, Seth D., and Alan B. Krueger. *A Proposal for Modernizing Labor Laws for Twenty-First-Century Work: The "Independent Worker."* The Hamilton Project. December 2015. http://www.hamiltonproject.org/assets/files/modernizing_labor_laws_for_twenty_first_century_work_krueger_harris.pdf.

12. Katz, Lawrence F., and Alan B. Krueger. "The Rise of Alternative Work Arrangements & the 'Gig' Economy." *Katz and Krueger Alt Work Deck* (Scribd slide deck). March 14, 2016. https://www.scribd.com/doc/306279776/Katz-and-Krueger-Alt-Work-Deck.

13. Zumbrun, Josh, and Anna Louie Sussman. "Proof of a 'Gig Economy' Revolution Is Hard to Find." *Wall Street Journal*, July 26, 2015. http://www.wsj.com/articles/proof-of-a-gig-economy-revolution-is-hard-to-find-1437932539.

14. Copeland, Craig. "Employee Tenure Trends, 1983–2014." *ERBI.org Notes* 36, no. 2 (February 2015): 2–3.

15. Chartered Institute of Personnel and Development. *Megatrends: The Trends Shaping Work and Working Lives*. July 2013. https://www.cipd.co.uk/Images/megatrends_2013-job-turnover-slowed-down_tcm18-11402.pdf.

PART II
The Reason for Being and the Three Employee Experience Environments

Organizations seeking to create amazing employee experiences need to start with a Reason for Being, which acts as the foundation for the three employee experience environments—technology, the physical space, and culture. In this section of the book, we will look at what all of these components are, examples of what organizations are doing in these respective areas, and some things that you might be able to do at your organization.

CHAPTER 4

Reason for Being

We've all heard of mission statements that typically set out to explain the purpose of the organization. Oftentimes they talk about being the market leader, providing shareholder value, delivering superior customer experience, or something else along these lines. Although these statements may talk about what the organization is trying to do, they don't go beyond that to make the leap from business to human. These statements or ideas do little to inspire employees (or anyone else for that matter) or to encourage action. Organizations that deliver amazing employee experiences transcend this basic concept of a mission statement by connecting what the organization does to the people who are actually affected. In other words, it answers the question "What impact does the organization have on the world and on the community around it?" This isn't about shareholder value, customer service, or profits, so you won't find any of these things mentioned. A great Reason for Being is also something that is unattainable, which forces the organization to keep thinking and dreaming big. Last, this needs to be something that rallies employees and ignites them; why should they care and why should they stand by you? You can see the four attributes of a Reason for Being in figure 4.1 below.

In a *New York Times* article titled "The Incalculable Value of Finding a Job You Love," Robert H. Frank, a professor of Cornell University, stated, "One of the most important dimensions of job satisfaction is how you feel about your employer's mission."[1] This is based on a book he wrote called *What Price the Moral High Ground?* This, of course, should

Focuses on the impact on the world and people

Is not centered on financial gain

Is something unattainable

Rallies employees

JACOB MORGAN
© thefutureorganization.com

FIGURE 4.1   A Reason for Being

come as no surprise, but it should also force us to move beyond typical mission statements.

Look at the following statements and ask yourself whom they belong to and how they make you feel. Do these read like typical mission statements or Reasons for Being? The differences are quite stark. Which companies would you rather work for?

STATEMENTS FROM LEADING ORGANIZATIONS

People working together as a lean, global enterprise for automotive leadership, as measured by: Customer, Employee, Dealer, Investor, Supplier, Union/Council, and Community Satisfaction.
Belong Anywhere.

[Company name] is committed to our customers and employees, and dedicated to delivering the highest levels of satisfaction in the implementation and ongoing support of our solutions.

To be a leader in the distribution and merchandising of food, pharmacy, health and personal care items, seasonal merchandise, and related products and services.

To refresh the world, to inspire moments of optimism and happiness, and to create value and make a difference.

To inspire and nurture the human spirit—one person, one cup and one neighborhood at a time.

To offer the finest service that assures customer satisfaction with cost efficient structure and shortest delivery time.

To be the leading supplier of semiconductor fabrication solutions worldwide—through innovation and enhancement of customer productivity with systems and service solutions.

To organize the world's information and make it universally accessible and useful.

Use our pioneering spirit to responsibly deliver energy to the world

You can go through these and clearly tell the difference between organizations that are following the mission statement 101 guide and organizations that are creating a Reason for Being. Here's the list of companies mentioned above (in order).

Ford
Airbnb
McKesson
Kroger
Coca-Cola
Starbucks
EY
Applied Materials
Google
ConocoPhillips

You can think of the Reason for Being as the umbrella that covers the three employee experience environments. Employee experience starts from there and affects the physical space, technology, and culture of the organization.

Salesforce.com does an excellent job of this. Its Reason for Being states:

> Salesforce.org is based on a simple idea: leverage Salesforce's technology, people, and resources to help improve communities around the world. We call this integrated philanthropic approach the 1-1-1 model because it started with a commitment to leverage 1% of Salesforce's technology, people, and resources to improve communities around the world. By encouraging and enabling companies to adopt the 1-1-1 model, Salesforce.org is helping to spark a worldwide corporate giving revolution.

This statement clearly focuses on the impact on the world (improve communities around the world), is not centered on financial gain (in fact the only mention of anything around money deals with how much it gives, not how much it gets), is something unattainable (there are countless communities around the world), and definitely rallies employees who want to make a difference.

Very few organizations around the world incorporate their philanthropic efforts directly into the goal of the company and why it actually exists, especially if this isn't a part of their core business. Salesforce.com has become known around the world not just as a technology company but also as an organization that wants to improve the world. This belief and philosophy has been with the company since its creation decades ago and is one of the reasons why Saleforce was among the top scoring companies featured in this book.

From here we can start to look at an organization's Employee Experience Score (ExS), which is determined by looking at 17 variables inside of an organization. These are the 17 things that employees care about most when it comes to technology, physical workplace, and culture:

- Consumer grade technology
- Technology availability
- Technology focusing on employee needs

- Workplace options
- Values reflected in the physical space
- Being proud to bring in friends or visitors
- Workplace flexibility and autonomy
- A sense of purpose
- Fair treatment
- Feeling valued
- Managers acting like coaches and mentors
- Feeling like you're part of a team
- Ability to learn something new, advance, and get the resources to do both
- Referring others to work at your organization
- Diversity and inclusion
- Health and wellness
- Brand perception

You can see the actual questions used to evaluate the ExS in the Appendix, where you can see how your organization ranks. You can also check out https://TheFutureOrganization.com to see the full rankings and to take the assessment online. These 17 attributes are what the most forward-thinking and progressive organizations around the world are investing in. As you read more about each one of these variables, you will also notice that they uncover more than what appears on the surface. For example, looking at things such as being proud to bring in friends or visitors or feeling a sense of purpose at the organization reveals things that are not directly asked in the survey, such as having a connection to the organization or feeling excitement about the brand. You will see many of these as you read more about the 17 variables.

Out of the 252 organizations that I ranked and evaluated for all of these variables, only 15 of them can be considered Experiential Organizations, that is, the very best at providing employee experiences. In order of rank these 15 organizations are:

1. Facebook
2. Apple
3. Google
4. LinkedIn

5. Ultimate Software
6. Airbnb
7. Microsoft
8. Riot Games
9. Accenture
10. Salesforce.com
11. Hyland Software
12. Cisco
13. Amazon
14. Adobe
15. World Wide Technology

These comprise just 6 percent of the organizations I analyzed, which shows that there is still a tremendous amount of growth and opportunity for organizations around the world to focus on employee experience. So what is it that these organizations are doing that others aren't, and perhaps more important, what's the value of investing in employee experience? Many of the examples in this book will be of these leading organizations that I analyzed. However, there will also be a few examples of organizations that I didn't analyze but whose executives I had the opportunity to get to know and speak with, which I believe are also doing unique things around employee experience.

In the next few chapters I'll explore what the 17 attributes actually mean, what they measure, and what organizations are doing related to these attributes. An entire book can easily be devoted to each one of the 17 attributes (and some have books about them). I want to stress that it is not my intention to provide a strategy for each one of these 17 variables. I simply want to convey why and how they are a part of the overall employee experience.

THE THREE EMPLOYEE EXPERIENCE ENVIRONMENTS

Although employee experience can appear to be a daunting and somewhat nebulous concept, you should take comfort in knowing that anything and everything your organization does now and in the future will

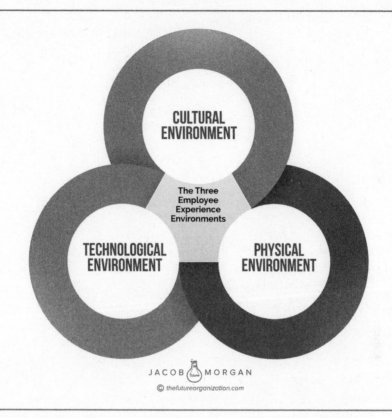

FIGURE 4.2   The Three Employee Experience Environments

fall into just three potential environments, which represent technology, the physical space, and your culture (see Figure 4.2). Let's look at each one these in more detail and look at the specific variables that make them up.

NOTE

1. Frank, Robert H. "The Incalculable Value of Finding a Job You Love." *New York Times*, July 22, 2016. http://www.nytimes.com/2016/07/24/upshot/first-rule-of-the-job-hunt-find-something-you-love-to-do.html?_r=0.

CHAPTER 5

The Physical Environment

The physical environment is the one in which employees actually work, and it comprises 30 percent of the employee experience. This is our surroundings and includes everything from the art that hangs on the wall to the catered meals the organization may offer to the cubicles or open floor plan employees may sit in. It's no secret why our physical space matters. We all want to spend our workdays in environments that energize and inspire us. These types of workspaces help us feel more creative, engaged, and connected to the company we work for. Not only that but also the physical environments in which we work act as symbols that represent the organization and our decision to be there. Great physical environments act as positive symbols and representations. Poor physical spaces act as negative ones. This was first discovered by Edgar Schein, a former professor at the Massachusetts Institute of Technology (MIT) Sloan School of Management and author of the book *Organizational Culture and Leadership*. In this book he talks about three levels of organizational culture, which are artifacts, values, and assumptions. According to Schein, all three of these things must align, and there are a lot of parallels between these three levels and the three employee experience environments that are explored in this book.

Interestingly enough, with the rise of coworking locations, global connectivity, and collaboration technologies, many people believe that offices are going to die. This is only somewhat true. The traditional idea of an office is indeed going to die—the one with gray walls, brown carpets, and lines of cubicle farms. However, the buildings themselves are going through a bit of an office design renaissance, and instead of disappearing, offices are reemerging as employee experience centers. According to commercial real estate firm CBRE, commercial real estate (at least in the United States) is at a seven-year high, and organizations such as Amazon, Cisco, Samsung, Whirlpool, General Electric, Schneider Electric, Deloitte, Microsoft, LinkedIn, and many others are investing many millions of dollars into creating these employee experience centers, for a very good reason. As the world of work continues to evolve and change, so do the environments in which the work actually gets done.

It's like redesigning a car by upgrading the engine and leaving the interior the same—it might be more powerful but if it's not pleasant to spend time in, you won't want to drive it! A recent study by furniture manufacturer Steelcase called "The Privacy Crisis" found that nearly 90 percent of workers around the world are less than satisfied with their work environments, which means that there is a lot of room for improvement.[1]

In 2010 *British Journal of Management* published a study by Craig Knight and S. Alexander Haslam from Exeter University called "Your Place or Mine? Organizational Identification and Comfort as Mediators of Relationships Between the Managerial Control of Workspace and Employees' Satisfaction and Well-Being." In the study they found that there is a social identity that employees have with their workspaces, and the physical environment can affect the psychological comfort of the employees who work there.

To create a great physical environment for employees, organizations need to focus on the following major characteristics, which are abbreviated as COOL (see Figure 5.1):

- Chooses to bring in friends or visitors
- Offers flexibility
- Organization's values are reflected
- Leverages multiple workspace options

FIGURE 5.1 COOL Office Spaces

CHOOSES TO BRING IN FRIENDS OR VISITORS

Why do organizations such as Airbnb, LinkedIn, Zappos, and Google let you bring your friends or family members to work? Facebook actually lets any employee bring up to four visitors at any time to see the campus, eat, and hang out. This is actually encouraged. But for what? It certainly takes time, effort, and resources to host and guide people around who don't actually work there so why make the investment?

It turns out there's a lot you can learn about an organization that is willing to open up its doors to others. From what I have observed, these types of organizations tend to have more focus on overall employee well-being, create a sense of community and diversity, drive innovation, and do a better job of connecting what the organization does back to the employees. In a sense, they have to because they are living and working in a metaphorical glass house that anyone can see into. These companies invest heavily in creating great employee experiences, which is why they feel confident opening their doors. They are holding themselves accountable.

As I mentioned above our offices are evolving into employee experience centers—museum-like places where employees can feel a sense of awe, curiosity, inspiration, joy, and pride. We all want to feel proud of the spaces we work in. The physical workspace helps create a connection between the organization and the employees who work there. Ultimately the physical environment is a reflection of the values of the organization (which is another key criterion of designing employee experiences discussed later in this chapter). Employees who work in great physical environments typically feel a sense of pride and joy when it comes to their office space. They want to show it off when they are given the opportunity to do so.

When I was younger I worked for various organizations in roles that included a grocery clerk, telemarketer, movie theater usher, marketing analyst, and strategy consultant. When I worked at Whole Foods Market as a grocery clerk, I would always be proud when people walked into my so-called office. It was always well organized, clean, and modern looking. Interestingly enough, years later when I worked as a consultant for a 400,000-person company, I would have dreaded for any of my friends or family members to come visit me in my dreary cubicle. To this day I look back at my fond memories of working at Whole Foods, which I consider one of the best jobs I've ever had.

One of the easiest and most effective ways an organization can get a sense of whether employees feel proud of their workspaces and a connection to the organization is by seeing whether employees bring in their friends and family members when and if allowed. Funny enough, you rarely hear about a company with an unattractive work environment offering something like this! I always encourage organizations to open their doors to friends, family members, and strangers if possible. Let people take tours, speak with employees, and get a sense of what it's like to work there.

If your organization is uncomfortable doing so, then chances are that the environment in which employees work is not seen as something to be proud of (assuming you don't have any legal issues preventing people from coming into the office).

In addition, opening your doors can also be a great talent and recruitment strategy, assuming that you have an inspiring environment where your employees work. It's why so many business leaders from around the world flock to Silicon Valley to see what the organizations there are doing.

If you have a great physical workspace, why wouldn't you want to show it to others? You can bet that when nonemployees walk through the door and think, "Man, this must be a cool place to work," they will be checking out your job listings page when they get home. Of course, the opposite is also true, which is why the physical space is so important.

The rationale behind looking at this variable as a function of employee experience is quite straightforward. If employees feel like they work in a beautiful and modern environment, they will typically leverage the opportunity to show it to visitors and friends. Do you have the confidence to open your doors to others?

What This Measures

- Pride in the employee's workplace
- Excitement about the organization
- Connection between employees and the organization

What You Can Do

- Open up your organization to friends and family members of employees and even the public who might want to do a tour (assuming you have a space worth looking at; if not, that's a bigger issue!).
- Think of your physical environment as an employee experience center instead of as an office.

See Table 5.1 to see who some of the highest- and lowest-scoring companies for this variable are.

TABLE 5.1 Chooses to Bring in Friends or Visitors

Some Highest-Scoring Organizations	Some Lowest-Scoring Organizations
Apple	Gilead Sciences
Facebook	World Fuel Services
LinkedIn	Safeway
Riot Games	Sears

OFFERS FLEXIBILITY

I explored this in considerable depth in my previous book, *The Future of Work*. Workplace flexibility continues to be a massive area of desire for employees and focus for organizations. We live in a hyperconnected global world where work-life balance has been obliterated and replaced by work-life integration. This means we take our personal lives to work and our work lives home. To continue to work in this type of environment, we have to abandon the notion of the 9 to 5 workday and instead shift toward allowing employees to work anytime from locations of their choosing whenever possible. Granted, this type of work environment is not suited or available for every type of role, for example manufacturing. Still, employees should have as much flexibility and choice as possible.

Consider the following statistics from Global Workplace Analytics:

- Half of the U.S. workforce has jobs in which at least partial telework is possible, and one-quarter to one-fifth of the workforce works remotely with some frequency.
- Eighty percent to 90 percent of U.S. employees would like to telework part-time at minimum. Two or three days per week appears to be the right amount, allowing enough time for on-site collaborative work and off-site concentrative work.
- Because studies show employees are away from their desk as much as 60 percent of their workday, Fortune 1000 companies worldwide are entirely redesigning their space.[2]

However, workplace flexibility doesn't simply mean letting employees work from home. Flexibility refers to employees genuinely being able to pick when and where they work whether it means coming into an office, working from home, going to a coffee shop or coworking facility, or going anywhere else where they can get their jobs done. According to FlexJobs, a site that allows employees to search for the best flexible work and telecommuting jobs, flexible work provides several benefits to employees and the organization, including:

- Increased productivity
- Less stressed employees
- Decreased absenteeism
- Healthier and happier employees
- Cost savings
- Increased trust

In 2016 *American Sociological Review* published a study called "Does a Flexibility/Support Organizational Initiative Improve High-Tech Employees' Well-Being? Evidence from the Work, Family, and Health Network." The lead authors are Phyllis Moen, who is the presidential chair in sociology at the University of Minnesota and Erin L. Kelly, a professor in work and organization studies at the MIT Sloan School of Management. In the study Moen et al. worked with a Fortune 500 company (not named) over a 12-month period to see whether workplace flexibility had any noticeable impact. To accomplish the study, they worked within the IT group, where they split them into two groups. One would have the flexible program and the other would not. The pilot group given the flexible work options was able to work anywhere and anytime and was evaluated based on the work produced instead of being seen in the office. The results of the study were quite conclusive, showing that the team within IT that was given the flexible work arrangement felt better about their jobs, had less burnout, and felt lower levels of stress. This was the first time a study of this type was conducted with a control and pilot group inside of a large organization. According to the authors, the study shows the necessity of organization-wide initiatives creating greater supervisor support and control and flexibility for employees.[3]

To further make this point, EY did a study in 2015 that surveyed almost 10,000 full-time employees in eight of the world's largest economies, which include the United States, Japan, Germany, the United Kingdom, Brazil, China, India, and Mexico. The employees listed flexibility as a top feature they wanted in a job and ranked it slightly less important than a competitive salary.[4]

Looking at how the workplace continues to change, it's almost impossible to imagine a world where workplace flexibility won't become the standard for how we work. It's simply becoming too hard, too stressful, and less practical not to have this type of arrangement. Not to mention we have the technologies today that can easily support this way of working.

I use Uber quite frequently when I travel not just in the United States but internationally as well. I always like to strike up a conversation with the drivers to find out why they work with Uber and why they like it. I've had drivers with all sorts of backgrounds ranging from airplane mechanics and corporate attorneys to nurses and finance MBA graduates. They are people who could easily be working for companies like Wells Fargo, Deloitte, or United Airlines, but they aren't. Why not? Because of the flexibility that Uber offers them, that's the number one thing every Uber driver always tells me. The amount of money they would make isn't that different, but they value being able to be in control of when and where they work. This is also what freelancers on sites such as Upwork always say as well; flexibility does indeed make a huge difference. This used to be seen as a perk or a bonus, but now many employees consider this the standard for how work could and should be done.

What This Measures

- Organization's willingness to adapt to how work gets done
- Commitment to employees to make their lives easier
- Progressive workplace thinking

What You Can Do

- Introduce a workplace flexibility program.
- Provide education and training to employees on why and how the flexibility program works.
- Set clear expectations and guidelines for the program.

TABLE 5.2   Offers Flexibility

Some Highest-Scoring Organizations	Some Lowest-Scoring Organizations
Cisco	Gilead Sciences
Mitre	AmerisourceBergen
SRC/SRCTec	Ingram Micro
Aflac	Arnold & Porter

See Table 5.2 to see who some of the highest- and lowest-scoring companies for this variable are.

ORGANIZATION'S VALUES ARE REFLECTED

Every organization has its own set of values, which are typically words or phrases the organization believes in or wants to represent. Values help guide the culture and the actions that the organization chooses to take. Oftentimes these values include words or phrases such as *trust, transparency, fun, innovation, collaboration,* and *honesty.* For many organizations these things (just like mission statements) are nothing more than lip service and useless platitudes. I see this time and time again in many organizations, and I'm sure you do as well.

A few years ago I was brought into a large company that wanted me to advise it on some issues related to employee experience. Naturally I was excited to do so. This particular organization had values that included some of the ones listed above. When an organization says its values are trust, fun, transparency, and so on, then typically I expect to see these values reflected in the actual workplace. However, in this particular instance I found the exact opposite. Employees all had to commute and work 9 to 5, there was no communication or collaboration going on, the workplace attire was extremely formal, the entire floor was colored brown and lined with giant cubicles, employees all looked unhappy, and the CEO's response to why he didn't want to change anything was "It was like that the day I got here and it will be like that the day I leave." Although the organization still exists I wasn't shocked to learn that some of its divisions have either filed for bankruptcy or have been sold off. There's really no kind way to put this, but as an organization if you say you care about and believe in something and your actions (especially internally) don't reflect that, then you are lying to yourself and to everyone who interacts with you.

If this particular organization were to be honest with itself, its values would have actually been don't communicate, keep outdated workplace practices, build the tallest hierarchy, make employees miserable, and do what you're told. It's not enough to have values, to communicate those values, or even to have employees memorize what those values are. Values need to be physically manifested in the spaces in which employees work (and ingrained in the culture, which I will explore later). In other words, if you were to walk around your organization, would you actually be able to see your values come to life?

Oftentimes when we interview to work for organizations, the question of values comes up. We have our personal values and the organization has its values. As employees we make decisions based on these sets of values because we want to work for an organization where they align. If you care about making the world a better place, being fit, being able to learn new things, contributing ideas to executives, and having fun, then naturally you would want to work for an organization that enables you to do so and cares about similar things. So what happens when you join a company and it doesn't actually manifest the values it says it cares about? You feel lied to, betrayed, and cheated. Unfortunately at that point you already signed the contract, so you can't really jump ship. Immediately you become resentful.

Your home can say a lot about who you are. Everything from the paintings or photographs you hang on the wall to the color of the walls to the type of dining table to even the types of towels and soaps you put in the bathrooms speaks. When you walk into someone's home, you get a better sense of who someone is, and when you walk into organization, you get a better sense of the type of organization it really is.

Facebook, which scored highest out of all 252 organizations on the Employee Experience Index, has five core values, which are "Be

Bold, Focus on Impact, Move Fast, Be Open, and Build Social Value." Definitely a noble set of values to have. If you visit the Facebook campus, you can quite literally see the manifestation of these values. Whether it's the mainly open floor plan, the eclectic art that adorns the workplace, the ability of employees to quickly move around the campus to work anywhere they want, the diverse group of employees (each with his or her unique fashion style), the guest business leaders who come speak to the employees, the customer stories that are shared, or the fact that employees are encouraged to speak up to share their ideas and feedback and even challenge their managers—you can absolutely see the values come to life.

I was at an executive customer board meeting for a large technology company not too long ago. One of the attendees mentioned that one of his company's core values was "Do the right thing" and asked how they could possibly show that value manifested in the workplace. I was honestly a bit stuck. Then another attendee chimed in that his organization also had this as one of the core values and brought this to life by having on-site battery recycling, charitable contributions, and guest speakers from social impact organizations and by consistently promoting ethical and sustainable business practices to employees. This is an amazing way to help employees see this value come to life!

Culture and technology take some time to absorb and get a feel for, but the physical space is something you can see and immediately make a judgment about. Remember, the physical space acts as a type of symbol for the organization and as a modern-day employee experience center or a museum for the people who work there. This is why one of the quickest ways to ruin an employee experience is by the organization not reflecting the values in the physical work environment. If you want to get a good sense of an organizational culture, then start by looking around at the workplace. It's something we can spot and notice on day one!

What This Measures

- Commitment to employees versus lip service for employees
- Whether the organization represents itself in the way it says it does
- Organizational honesty and integrity
- Culture

TABLE 5.3   Organization's Values Are Reflected

Some Highest-Scoring Organizations	Some Lowest-Scoring Organizations
Nike	General Dynamics
Google	AmerisourceBergen
Facebook	Archer Daniels Midland
Apple	Anthem

What You Can Do

- Write down your values on a sheet of paper and walk around the office. Do you see those values come to life? Why or why not?
- If the values do align, think about what you can do to enable everyone else at your organization to see that alignment. If they don't align, what can you do to fix that?

See Table 5.3 to see who some of the highest- and lowest-scoring companies for this variable are.

LEVERAGE MULTIPLE WORKSPACE OPTIONS

There has been an ongoing debate around open versus closed office spaces and which one is better. Open offices tend to enable collaboration, yet they are also prone to cause distractions and noise. Closed offices and cubicles tend to allow for more focused work, but they can also be a bit depressing while not encouraging collaboration and communication. So which one do you go with?

Unfortunately all of these debates and arguments around open versus closed offices miss the point entirely. The physical environment needs to be thought of as a house. Every room in a house is designed for a specific purpose. You eat in the dining room, cook in the kitchen, sleep in the bedroom, and relax in the living room.

Leesman is a company based in the United Kingdom that seeks to understand the relationship among organizations, people, and place.

It has studied and surveyed over 110,000 people and found that there are actually 21 workplace activities that employees participate in. These range from planned meetings to individual focused work to collaborating to relaxing and taking a break.[5] Clearly not all of these activities are effectively done in a single type of a space. It doesn't really make sense to relax and take a break in the same space that you have your planned meetings. Similarly, it doesn't make sense to eat and sleep in the kitchen.

Employees need access to environments that enable them to do their best work. This is in the best interest of the organization and of the employees who work there. We are moving away from working in a linear, monotonous world, so our workspaces must adapt accordingly. This is why the most forward-thinking organizations around the world are actually creating multiple floor plans instead of focusing on just open or closed spaces. None of the forward-thinking organizations in the world commit to just a single type of workspace environment (or even two or three!). For example, when I visited the offices of SAP, I noticed that they have a very wide variety of spaces that employees can choose to work from. This included modern cubicle-like environments, open spaces, cafe and lounge areas, collaboration spaces where you can write on the wall, conference rooms, quiet areas, outside work areas, and more. By creating this type of environment, organizations like SAP are saying, "We get it. Your job is not linear and uniform, so we will understand how and why you work and give you multiple options based on that. As an employee you should be able to pick the environment that will allow you to be most effective and efficient." That's a powerful message and a commitment to people. Many organizations also realize that they are able to save a lot of office space and hence real-estate cost by doing this because they are able to leverage those closed offices, usually devoted for a single person, for multiple people.

A recent article published in *Harvard Business Review* by Diane Hoskins, the co-CEO of architecture design firm Gensler, called "Employees Perform Better When They Control Their Space" found that employees who have more choices over their workplace (including when, where, and how they work) scored higher on innovation, job performance, job satisfaction, and workplace satisfaction. This makes complete sense. Why shouldn't we have a bit more control and choice over the spaces in which we work?

Perhaps one of the best examples of an organization that offers multiple workspace options is the commercial real estate company CBRE, which redesigned its Los Angeles offices to focus on "16 spaces to work." Think about that for a minute. Most employees are lucky if they are afforded a way to work beyond their cubicles, but 16 spaces is really astonishing. CBRE is in the process of pushing this out to its other offices as well. These spaces include everything from a client conference room and open team areas to teamwork tables and offices for a day to phone booths and even a Zen garden area. Each of these spaces caters to a specific way that employees at CBRE work.[6]

I recently spoke with Freddie Chow, the chief talent officer for the Asia Pacific Region of Sanofi. He told me that in his region, the physical environment employees work in creates and promotes a certain type of hierarchy. The more senior people get the nicer offices with the better desks and the more extravagant views. Sanofi was trying to become a more collaborative and flatter organization, so the physical environment was a big hindrance to making any kind of progress. Freddie and his team made a radical change and eliminated all the offices in the organization. Instead they focused their efforts on something known as Activity Based Working, which is a concept where employees don't have any assigned seats. Instead they have multiple floor plan and workspace options they can select from based on the activity or task they are doing. After this shift Freddie and his team saw an increase in productivity, engagement, and collaboration, along with a reduction in real estate costs.

Don't get stuck in the open versus closed office debate. Instead seek to understand the various activities that employees perform throughout the day and how they work. Then design spaces accordingly.

A word of caution when thinking about the physical workspace. When we see or hear about organizations like Google or Facebook, one of the first things we think about is their amazing office spaces. Business leaders flock from all over the world to visit these organizations in an attempt to bring back some things they can implement at their own companies. The thought process is "Google has a giant slide. We need one too!" Or "Facebook has a giant cafeteria with free food. We have to get that!" What many of these people fail to realize is that you can't simply copy a Google or a Facebook, nor should you. These organizations might seem like they are just building anything that looks fun, but everything they do in relation to their physical environment is done strategically and with purpose. Organizations that invest in beautiful spaces don't just do it for fun.

Atlassian is one of the cool and hip companies that have a modern and beautiful office space. I met with its executive team to find out whether they just hired a design firm and threw money at making an awesome-looking space. They laughed at me when I asked that. Atlassian actually analyzed how employees worked by using sensors attached to employee's desks and speaking with employees. After looking at the data executives realized that employees hardly used assigned seating, which led them to design a space that made sense for them, a more open central plan that leveraged multiple other ways of working.

Atlassian, like many other forward-thinking companies, didn't copy what others were doing. It used data to understand how employees work. Atlassian then designed around that.

Another executive I spoke with at a large organization didn't have a large budget to redesign the workspaces so he recruited volunteers. He set a budget at IKEA (the do-it-yourself furniture store), and everyone showed up for a few weekends to create environments they wanted to work in. Airbnb used to work with fancy design and architecture firms to build and design their conference rooms (which are modeled after actual Airbnb listings). Today the company recruits volunteer employees and gives them a $900 budget to design these conference rooms. Not only is this cheaper for Airbnb but employees also feel a sense of pride and ownership in actually creating the rooms.

You will be amazed how excited and engaged employees will be if you tell them they can design their own environments. Not only that but also I'm willing to bet that your organization has a few creative and handy employees who will know more than their fair share when it comes to design and furniture.

TABLE 5.4   Leverage Multiple Workspace Options

Some Highest-Scoring Organizations	Some Lowest-Scoring Organizations
Google	Sears
Facebook	McDonald's
LinkedIn	General Dynamics
Airbnb	Lowe's

What This Measures

- Commitment to enabling employees to do their best work
- Understanding of how employees work

What You Can Do

- Observe how employees work and where they work.
- Get employee feedback around the types of environments they would like to use.
- Think beyond open or closed floor plans, and instead view your organization like a house, where each room serves a specific and unique purpose.

See Table 5.4 to see who some of the highest- and lowest-scoring companies for this variable are.

HOW ORGANIZATIONS SCORED

The maximum number of points that an organization could have received for each of the above variables was 6.5 for a total of 26 possible points. Out of the four variables here, the one with the lowest average (4.3/6.5) was "The organization offers flexible work options (such as the ability to work your own hours wherever you want) and encourages autonomy." I found this rather surprising because workplace flexibility and autonomy have been two topics of discussion in the business world for many years, yet there is enormous room for improvement. The variable with

TABLE 5.5   Entire Physical Environment

Some Highest-Scoring Organizations	Some Lowest-Scoring Organizations
LinkedIn	General Dynamics
Apple	AmerisourceBergen
Facebook	United Technologies
Riot Games	Sears

the highest average (4.9/6.5) was "The physical space reflects the values of the organization (e.g., if the values are collaboration, openness, transparency, and fun, then you wouldn't expect to see a dull environment with nothing but cubicles!)." Although the score here is still relatively low, I believed that most organizations would struggle with this physical space variable the most. Surprisingly that was not the case.

On average, the 252 organizations I analyzed scored a 4.6 for each question, or 18.4/26 for the physical space environment. This just barely comes to 71 percent of the maximum that an organization can get. If this were the University of Employee Experience, then collectively these organizations would get a C− for their physical environment grade.

Having a COOL workplace is more than just having some color on the walls, a beer keg, and free food. It's more than visiting a Silicon Valley company and copying what it does. Organizations that create truly COOL workspaces genuinely understand how and why employees work and design spaces that reflect those ways of working. Only then will the physical environment truly help create an overall positive employee experience. Budget is also not an excuse for why organizations aren't able to rethink their physical environment.

When looking at the entire physical environment, here are some examples of the highest- and lowest-scoring organizations (see Table 5.5).

NOTES

1. Steelcase. "The Privacy Crisis." *360 Magazine*, no. 68, November 12, 2014. https://www.steelcase.com/insights/articles/privacy-crisis/.

2. Global Workplace Analytics. "Latest Telecommuting Statistics." January 2016. http://globalworkplaceanalytics.com/telecommuting-statistics.
3. Moen, Phyllis, Erin Kelly, Wen Fan, Shi-Rong Lee, David Almeida, Ellen Kossek, and Orfeu Buxton. "Does a Flexibility/Support Organizational Initiative Improve High-Tech Employees' Well-Being? Evidence from the Work, Family, and Health Network." *American Sociological Review* 81, no. 1 (2016). doi:10.1177/0003122415622391.
4. EY. *Global Generations: A Global Study on Work-Life Challenges across Generations: Detailed Findings.* 2015. http://www.ey.com/Publication/vwLUAssets/EY-global-generations-a-global-study-on-work-life-challenges-across-generations/$FILE/EY-global-generations-a-global-study-on-work-life-challenges-across-generations.pdf.
5. Rothe, Peggie. "Flexibility and Variety Hold the Key as Employees' Activity Profiles Become More Complex." *Leesman Review* no. 18 (September 2015): 4–7.
6. Moore, Beth, and Paul Scialla. "WELL Certified Workplaces—The Next Generation of Sustainability." Workplace Evolutionaries webinar slides. 2014. cdn.ifma.org/crec/webinars/ifma-webinar_wellness-jan-2014.pdf?sfvrsn=0.

CHAPTER 6

The Technological Environment

In 2016 I delivered a talk to a large organization where I explored how the workplace is changing. After my talk I held some candid discussions where employees could share pretty much anything they wanted with me. In almost every conversation I had employees told me how much they loved the people whom they worked with and the work they did. Still, many of them were extremely frustrated and unhappy with the company they were a part of. Several were already interviewing elsewhere. Naturally my response was "Why would you want to leave an organization where you love the people and the work?" At this particular company the answer was technology. Employees were extremely frustrated with the tools they were using to get their jobs done. Information would go missing, it would take too many steps to complete simple tasks, things would freeze up, and the interfaces were quite literally from the 1980s.

This made their jobs much harder to do, which in turn caused employees to get upset with one another and resent the organization for not doing anything to improve the situation.

Although we view technology as something that lives in a separate nonhuman bucket, technology has a palpable impact on the organization—it's what we use to communicate, collaborate, and actually get our jobs done. If the tools break down, then everything else around them, including the human relationships, also breaks down.

The technological environment includes everything from the apps you use to the hardware and software to the user interface and design. Any technologies you use to get your job done are a part of the technological environment, whether they be videoconferencing platforms, internal social networks, task management tools, human resources (HR) software, billing and invoicing systems, or anything in between. This is also where we typically hear the phrase *digital transformation* mentioned as organizations struggle to apply these technologies to all aspects of how employees work.

Technology is what helps enable much of the future of work and employee experience—it acts as the glue and the nervous system that power the organization. To improve the overall employee experience, organizations must create an ACE technological environment. If you're interested in learning more about technology deployments (specifically those related to social collaboration), I wrote a 340-page book specifically about this topic called *The Collaborative Organization* which came out in 2012.

To create a great technological environment for employees, organizations need to focus on the following major characteristics, which are abbreviated as ACE (see Figure 6.1):

- Availability to everyone
- Consumer grade technology
- Employee needs versus business requirements

AVAILABILITY TO EVERYONE

Although many organizations have good intentions, they oftentimes segment and isolate certain employees who get access to new technologies. For example, the engineering team has a great new platform that only it is allowed to use. I've interviewed many employees who feel a bit neglected when they know that their peers are getting access to technologies that they don't have access to. And why can't they access these new technologies? "It wasn't approved for everyone." Employees are the ones doing the actual work, so they should clearly have a say in the types

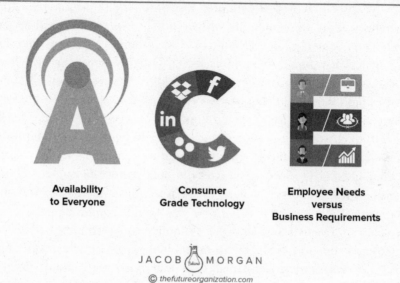

Availability to Everyone   **Consumer Grade Technology**   **Employee Needs versus Business Requirements**

JACOB MORGAN
© thefutureorganization.com

FIGURE 6.1 ACE Technology

of technologies that they are using, especially if another team or department already has access to it. Technology availability also becomes even more of an issue when we look at flexible work arrangements. Typically the teams that have the technologies in place to support flexible work (videoconferencing, internal social networks, task and project management tools, and the like) are the ones who actually get to take advantage of it.

It's not hard to see why this can cause problems, resentment, and frustration, thus negatively affecting the overall employee experience. Technology that is granted to one subset of employees should be made available to all if they want it and are aware of it. Organizations have long approached technology deployments from a multiyear pilot program standpoint, but all the chief information officers and chief technology officers I speak with agree that with the rapid pace of technological change, this type of model no longer works and isn't practical. By the time your organization settles on something it wants to roll out effectively, a few years will go by, the workforce won't look the same, and the technologies you are implementing will already be out of date. A study by *MIT Sloan Management Review* and Capgemini Consulting reported by Michael Fitzgerald, Nina Kruschwitz, Didier Bonnet, and Michael Welch called "Embracing Digital Technology: A New Strategic Imperative" found that 63 percent of respondents said the pace of technology change in their organization is too slow.[1]

Although some pilot projects are perfectly fine to have, long-term technology access to only a subset of employees actually does far more harm than good. One of the ways to make sure you create a great technological environment is by making the technologies available to everyone who works there.

The San Diego Zoo is 100-year-old nonprofit with a lofty goal of trying to end extinction. To date it has over 3,000 employees who range from cashiers to zoologists and botanists to animal trainers and office workers. It's one of the most diverse organizations in existence. I spent some time with Tim Mulligan, chief human resources officer, and Steisha Ponczoch, HR manager, to learn more about how the zoo can possibly equip such a diverse workforce with technology. Surely if it can do it, anyone can.

Not that long ago all the training and education that was done at the San Diego Zoo was done in classrooms with books, binders, and note taking. The company didn't even allow employees to be on their cell phones while on the job. It has come a long way since then! Today it has a robust online training and learning management system that allows employees to learn on their own time. Any employee (including the animal trainers) can access essential training for free at their fingertips from any computer, including those provided in the two Learning Labs that Tim and his team have created for staff use.

A few years ago a strategic decision was made to go paperless, and since then all personnel files are stored online where they can be accessed when needed. All HR forms are now completed electronically as well, including onboarding paperwork, which, in the first year of implementation, eliminated over 100,000 sheets of paper for that process alone. This move has since inspired other departments to archive and process paperlessly, helping the zoo conserve natural resources.

Beyond using technology for work, Mulligan developed a program to provide even greater access to technology that employees can use in their personal lives as well. The Z-Tech program offers interest-free payroll deductions on dozens of the latest tech products, such as computers, cameras, tablets, printers, smart watches, and even gaming consoles. This incredibly successful program has helped hundreds of employees, who otherwise either may not have had the funds up front to purchase them or may have gotten stuck with high-interest financing, gain access to technology.

In today's world there is really no excuse for why every employee at your company can't have access to technology.

What This Measures

- Commitment to driving innovation, collaboration, and communication across the organization
- Focus on enabling the organization as a whole
- Technological adeptness

What You Can Do

- Whenever possible default to giving employees more access, not less.
- Be as transparent as you can with new technology decisions and deployments.

See Table 6.1, which shows some of the highest- and lowest-scoring companies for this variable.

TABLE 6.1 Availability to Everyone

Some Highest-Scoring Organizations	Some Lowest-Scoring Organizations
Facebook	World Fuel Services
Apple	Southern Ohio Medical Center
Google	Gilead Sciences
Riot Games	Gilbane

CONSUMER GRADE TECHNOLOGY

Over the past few years we've placed an unhealthy emphasis on deploying enterprise grade technologies. Although there is no standard definition of what this actually means, it usually refers to technology that is suited to the needs of a large organization versus being used by individuals or consumers (consumer grade technology). Ideally this means it's more robust, securer, more flexible, and more geared for IT professionals to manage and deploy. But really what this ends up meaning inside of large organizations is clunky, outdated software. I've seen many of these technologies, and I'm always amazed that people actually use them. I'm sure many readers of this book can relate.

I equate this to the organization buying a giant bulletproof tank when employees really want and need something more stylish, maneuverable, flexible, modern, and attractive. This is why so many new enterprise tools today are modeling themselves after technologies we use in our personal lives all the time (platforms such as Twitter, LinkedIn, Facebook, or Google). In a sense, the consumer technologies are becoming enterprise technologies. A simpler way for organizations to look at this is by giving tools to employees that actually look like they are designed for humans and not for rocket scientists or developers (yes, they are humans too!). My definition of a consumer grade technology is something that is so well designed, useful, and valuable that you would consider using something similar in your personal life if it existed.

Think of the file-sharing tools you use at work. Would you use something similar in your life to organize your personal information? What about the billing and invoice system you have? Would you use the same technology to organize your personal finances? What about your customer relationship management system? Would you store your contacts using the same technology? You can see the direction this is going in. We have access to so many amazing technologies and platforms in our personal lives, but for some reason when we show up to work, we are stuck using the same tools we used to use decades earlier. Imagine if you still had one of those old TVs at home where you had to get up and physically change the channel. What if you had a rotary phone in your home or an old IBM Commodore computer? (I've never seen one but I hear they were all the rage back in the day!)

This is why organizations like The Royal Bank of Scotland have rolled out Facebook at Work (the business version of Facebook) to over 100,000 employees. They recognize that employees use Facebook in their personal lives and want something that emulates that experience in the workplace. Roche, the 90,000-person company that specializes in research-focused health care, recently switched over to G Suite (formerly called Google for Work) for the same reasons. These are just two of the many organizations around the world that focus on giving employees tools that emulate the platforms and technologies they would use in their personal lives. There are a few benefits to doing this.

Most of the time when organizations deploy new, complex technology solutions, there's a lot of training and education that is required to teach employees how and why to use these new tools. Granted, education and training is needed for any type of change, but when employees are familiar with the technologies, they are much more likely to get up to speed quicker. Familiarity also removes complexity which means employees will actually use the tools. Consumer grade technologies are also more modern, more user friendly, and in general better looking than their traditional enterprise counterparts. Again this increases the likelihood of adoption, but it also has a bit of the *cool* factor, which employees certainly value and appreciate. Deploying consumer grade technologies is a big factor for the technological environment.

What This Measures

- Forward-thinking approach to technology across the organization
- Creating a modern work experience
- Enabling employees to be most effective and engaged in their jobs

What You Can Do

- Shift your thinking away from enterprise grade to consumer grade technologies.
- Look at the technologies employees use in their personal lives, and see what technological attributes you can bring into the organization.

TABLE 6.2   Consumer Grade Technology

Some Highest-Scoring Organizations	Some Lowest-Scoring Organizations
Microsoft	Honeywell
Apple	SAS
Google	Northwestern Mutual
Riot Games	Target

See Table 6.2, which shows some of the highest- and lowest-scoring companies for this variable.

EMPLOYEE NEEDS VERSUS BUSINESS REQUIREMENTS

Let's imagine for a moment that you walk into a car dealership and tell one of the sales representatives that you're looking for a car. He or she greets you and says, "Tell me what you're looking for?" and you respond by saying, "Well it needs to be able to fit five people, has to have great horsepower and torque, must be painted blue, and has to have all the new modern features of today's car." The dealer says, "Perfect, I have something for you." He or she then proceeds to wheel out a Frankenstein-like monstrosity that has five seats all on the left side of the car, a massive engine on the right side of the car, a steering wheel that's attached to the roof, and splotchy blue paint. "That will be $60,000. How do you want to pay?"

You're shocked! "I can't pay for this, that's not a car!"

"Sure it is. It has everything you wanted. See, I wrote it down here."

That's the difference between focusing on the needs of the employees versus the requirements of the business. Most IT departments simply go through a checklist of items instead of understanding how and why employees work. The problem with this, as outlined in the Frankencar example above, is that the way employees work rarely aligns with the technical checklist of the organization.

Typically the IT and the HR functions inside of organizations don't work together that closely. When it comes to designing employee experiences, this creates an amazing opportunity for these two roles to partner. IT needs to be more flexible and open to understanding the needs of the employees, but at the same time HR also needs to be aware of any potential issues that might surround any new technology deployment. I look at these two functions as chefs who are working together to create an amazing dish.

This creates a unique opportunity for business leaders in HR-related roles to partner and work with those in IT-related roles.

What This Measures

- Commitment to enabling employees to do their best work
- Listening to the voice of the employee

What You Can Do

- Start the HR and IT partnership conversation.
- Have IT include HR in some technology discussions, and have HR include IT in some of the people-centric discussions.

See Table 6.3, which shows some of the highest- and lowest-scoring companies for this variable.

TABLE 6.3   Employee Needs versus Business Requirements

Some Highest-Scoring Organizations	Some Lowest-Scoring Organizations
Microsoft	Hershey
Apple	Baptist Health South Florida
Google	World Fuel Services
Riot Games	Southern Ohio Medical Center

HOW ORGANIZATIONS SCORED

The maximum number of points that an organization could have received for each of the above variables was 6.5 for a total of 19.5 possible points. Out of the three variables here, the one with the lowest average (4.4/6.5) was "Generally, the technology employees use is focused on the needs of the employees instead of just on the technical requirements and specifications of the organization." This is something organizations have struggled with for a long time and I found this to be the case even in 2012 when I was writing *The Collaborative Organization*. Technology decisions continue to be made by looking at a feature or technology checklist as opposed to truly understanding how and why employees work. The variable with the highest average, even though it's still quite low scoring, (4.6/6.5) was "Generally, the technology that employees use is consumer grade (meaning it's so well designed, useful, and valuable that you would consider using something similar in your personal life if it existed)."

On average, the 252 organizations I analyzed scored a 4.5 for each question, or 13.5/19.5 for the technological environment. This comes to 69 percent of the maximum that an organization can get. Again, if this were the University of Employee Experience, then collectively these organizations would get a D+ for their technological environment grade.

Technology can be an amazing thing. It can either empower people or render them powerless. Organizations seeking to truly create employee experiences and design for the future of work cannot do so without having the proper tools in place. Everything from people analytics to collaboration to HR to flexible work is all powered by technology. Organizations that don't invest in the technological environment eventually hit a wall with how far and how fast they can adapt and innovate. When I think about the future of work, there are two functions that I believe are going to be the most impactful and are the most exciting. The first is HR and the second is IT. As I mentioned at the start of this book, technology is something that will affect every function of your organization, and every audience I have ever spoken in front of (and that's a lot!) agrees.

TABLE 6.4   Entire Technological Environment

Some Highest-Scoring Organizations	Some Lowest-Scoring Organizations
Apple	World Fuel Services
Facebook	SAS
Microsoft	Honeywell
Google	Sears

See Table 6.4, which shows some of the highest- and lowest-scoring companies for this variable.

NOTE

1. Fitzgerald, Michael, Nina Kruschwitz, Didier Bonnet, and Michael Welch. "Embracing Digital Technology: A New Strategic Imperative." *MIT Sloan Management Review*, October 7, 2013. http://sloanreview.mit.edu/projects/embracing-digital-technology/.

CHAPTER **7**

The Cultural Environment

Out of all the employees and business leaders whom I have interviewed over the years, the vast majority of them have always told me that culture is what they care about most. Unlike the previous two environments, the cultural environment isn't the one that you can see, touch, taste, or breathe in. This is the only environment that you feel. That feeling is the pit in your stomach when you don't want to go to work or the excitement and butterflies you get from wanting to go to work. Simply put, the cultural environment is the vibe of your organization and the actions that are taken to create that vibe or feeling.

The culture of the organization determines how employees are treated, the products or services that are created, the partnerships that are established, and even how employees actually get their jobs done. What's fascinating about culture, though, is that it exists regardless of whether the organization realizes it or decides to create it. A technological environment doesn't exist without actual things that the organization deploys. A physical environment doesn't exist unless the organization creates or designates one. But the corporate culture is like air. It's around all the employees who work there even if they aren't always aware of it. This is why it's so crucial to actually create and design a culture instead of just letting it exist. So what does the cultural environment actually look like?

There are 10 attributes that organizations must focus on to create a CELEBRATED culture (see Figure 7.1):

- Company is viewed positively
- Everyone feels valued
- Legitimate sense of purpose
- Employees feel like they're part of a team
- Believes in diversity and inclusion
- Referrals come from employees
- Ability to learn new things and given the resources to do so and advance
- Treats employees fairly
- Executives and managers are coaches and mentors
- Dedicated to employee health and wellness

COMPANY IS VIEWED POSITIVELY

Have you ever dated someone who you thought was a great catch, and then all of your friends and family members told you that they didn't like him or her (please tell me I'm not the only one)? Even if you thought this person was the one, you started to have doubts and reservations about this person. The same is true in the business world. If you start working for an organization that you believe to be a good fit and then hear about how much people don't like the company you are working for, you will start having doubts. This doesn't necessarily mean you will quit the company, but your overall employee experience will be affected negatively. I'm sure you can think of several examples of organizations that have treated animals cruelly, represented unethical business practices, harmed employees or the environment, or treated customers unfairly. Keep in mind that this isn't just about employees viewing the company positively but the public as well. We live in a very open and transparent world, so when an organization does something wrong or unethical, people tend to find out. Similarly when an organization is admired and revered, people want to work there.

C ompany Is Viewed Positively

E veryone Feels Valued

L egitimate Sense of Purpose

E mployees Feel Like They're Part of a Team

B elieves in Diversity and Inclusion

R eferrals Come from Employees

A bility to Learn New Things and Given Resources to Do So and Advance

T reats Employees Fairly

E xecutives and Managers Are Coaches and Mentors

D edicated to Employee Health and Wellness

JACOB MORGAN
© thefutureorganization.com

FIGURE 7.1 CELEBRATED Culture

Look at the most recent Fortune list of the World's Most Admired Companies:

1. Apple
2. Alphabet (parent company of Google)
3. Amazon
4. Berkshire Hathaway
5. Walt Disney
6. Starbucks
7. Southwest Airlines
8. FedEx
9. Nike
10. General Electric

Chances are that when you look at this list, you aren't surprised to see these organizations.

Sometimes organizations aren't viewed positively because they are simply engaging in poor business practices, but other times organizations don't do a good enough job of letting the world know what they stand for, why they do what they do, and what it's like to work there. In either case the situation needs to be corrected.

Dell does a great job of telling its story to the world, and to learn more about what it does, I spoke with Jennifer Newbill, senior manager, global candidate attraction, engagement, and experience. At Dell employees can go through a social media and brand certification program that enables them to become brand ambassadors of the company. These ambassadors feel a greater connection to the company, and they help share the Dell story and purpose, what it's like to work there, news and announcements, and much more. They feel like true representatives of the organization. Not only do these brand ambassadors make the rest of the world more aware of what Dell is doing and working on, but also these individuals have a higher employee Net Promoter Score (eNPS) than others at the company.

You may have heard of the website Glassdoor. I used their data as a source for the analysis in this book. Glassdoor is a website that provides an amazing amount of transparency into virtually any organization. Simply visit the website and type in your company name. Of course, not every company in the world is listed there but many are. You'll be able to see the overall company rating on a five-star scale, the CEO approval rating, salary information, candid reviews of the organization, pictures of the offices, the benefits, the interview process, and much more. The amazing thing is that this information is put up on the site by employees! So imagine you're looking to work for an organization. Before even submitting a resume you basically have all the information you need to decide whether this is a place you want to work for. Of course, Glassdoor is one example and is perhaps the best and most transparent company and career website in existence.

I used to think that lists that highlight the best or greatest companies to work for were a bit foolish and had no real business merit. However, although I might not always agree entirely with how and why all of these lists are created, I acknowledge that they have an impact on the overall brand perception of the organization and an impact on the overall employee experience. Employees feel a greater sense of pride when they are working for one of these awarded organizations, and from my observations it also appears that they stay there longer. What's interesting about these lists and awards is that some of them are quite hard to get onto and require significant financial and people resources. In other words to get the award or to make the list, you genuinely have to make some changes in your organization, which is a good thing. There are many of these lists and awards that are given, which include most admired companies, most sustainable, best or great places to work, happiest places to work, greenest companies, and so on.

Today, this company perception often falls under something called *employer branding*. HR is responsible for all the people inside of the organization, and marketing is responsible for driving awareness of products, services, and the organization as a whole. It's not hard to see why these two roles need to come together to focus on the overall company perception. Lydia Abbot, Ryan Batty, and Stephanie Bevegni's *Global Recruiting Trends 2016* report found that almost 50 percent of HR professionals "share or contribute to employer branding with marketing."[1]

General Electric has a killer brand, but it, like many others, has realized that the brand isn't enough to get the best people to work there.

Company perception can have a tremendous impact on the business. A study by LinkedIn, which was summarized in a 2016 blog post by Wade Burgess called "Research Shows Exactly How Much Having a Bad Employer Brand Will Cost You," found the following:

- The cost of a bad reputation for a company with 10,000 employees could be as much as $7.6 million in additional wages.
- Employers who fail to invest in their reputation could be paying up to an additional $4,723 per employee hired.
- Nearly half of US professionals would entirely rule out taking a job with a company that exhibited the top three negative employer brand factors, no matter what pay raise they were offered. Even a pay raise of 10% would only tempt 28% of us to sign on the dotted line.
- Companies with most (3 in 5) of the qualities encompassing a positive employer brand can attract 41% of full-time US workers without any pay increase. This rises to 46% if they have all 5—job security, more professional development opportunities, the opportunity to work on a better team, an organization with the same values as you and an organization that is talked about positively by present or past employees.
- Companies with all 5 qualities can win over nearly half (49%) of those aged 18–34 and 46% of those aged 35–54 with no pay increase.[2]

However, this doesn't mean your goal should be simply to make every list that's out there. Sure, that would be nice, but instead it's far more important to understand what the organization wants to be known for and how it can effectively tell that story and build the employer brand around it.

What This Measures

- Organizational effectiveness around telling its story
- Impact that the organization is having on the world around it
- Employer branding
- Pride

What You Can Do

- Look on sites like Glassdoor to see how your company is perceived by people who work there.
- Keep a good pulse on the news and conversations happening about your organization.
- Encourage HR and your marketing teams to work together.
- See what honorary lists your organization can become a part of.

EVERYONE FEELS VALUED

Compensation and benefits, having employee voices heard, and employees being recognized for the work they do, all fall under "every feels valued." We will look at all of those components here.

Do you want to work for an organization where you don't feel valued? If your answer is yes, then you need to put this book down and look for something in the self-help category.

For the rest of you I'm assuming this is not the case, but still, imagine being part of this type of organization. How would you feel when you show up to work, and more important, would you even want to show up to work? I've worked in and visited these types of organizations, and after spending some time there I genuinely started to hate them and relive that moment in the film *Office Space* when someone sets fire to the company (not recommended). Keep in mind that feeling valued and appreciated are not the same thing. Typically feeling appreciated is more relevant to a specific project or task, and feeling valued is the overall and ongoing feeling that employees have. So, if you feel regularly appreciated, then you will in turn feel valued.

Value can be quite subjective—we are all unique creatures with different beliefs, aspirations, values, and expectations. Ultimately, the best

TABLE 7.1   Company Is Viewed Positively

Some Highest-Scoring Organizations	Some Lowest-Scoring Organizations
Google	World Fuel Services
Apple	Sears
LinkedIn	AIG
St. Jude Children's Research Hospital	Mondelēz International

way to understand what your employees value and care about is to ask them and get to know them more personally. With that caveat in mind there are some common things we all care about that help us feel valued in the workplace. You can look at table 7.1 to see who some of the highest and lowest scoring companies for this variable are.

COMPENSATION AND BENEFITS

Depending on the reports you read, compensation and benefits is either one of the most important or one of the least important things that employees care about. For example, a recent Society for Human Resources Management report called "2016 Employee Job Satisfaction and Engagement: Revitalizing a Changing Workforce" found that compensation and pay ranked number two when it came to overall job satisfaction.[3] However, if you look at research done by career website Indeed called "The Indeed Job Happiness Index 2016: Ranking the World for Employee Satisfaction," it found that compensation actually ranked last on the list of variables that employees consider when reporting on overall job satisfaction.[4] Two different studies done during the same year with very different results.

It would be a bit silly simply to discount the importance or value of fair compensation. I've talked to employees and executives who put compensation at the very top of their personal job satisfaction list, and I've talked to plenty of people who don't. Interestingly enough, not many people are willing to work for free, so compensation and benefits remains a topic of conversation and discussion for every employee.

Even when looking at organizations such as Netflix, which publicly released its culture slide deck a few years ago, it's clear that although it does offer all sorts of fun perks and rewards, it's also explicit in acknowledging that it pays employees well. I have found this to be the case across all organizations that are interested in exploring and designing employee experiences. It's very hard for employees to feel valued if they don't believe they are at least being paid what they are worth.

HAVING EMPLOYEE'S VOICES HEARD

The typical structure inside of many organizations is the pyramid where information, decision making, and power flow from the top down. Although we are starting to see this break down and flatten out, this shift will naturally take time. Because we are all so used to managers and executives controlling all the information and making all the decisions, this concept of employees having their voices heard can come as a challenge. Thanks to social media and the Internet in general, this process is now being forced to speed up. When it comes to the voice of the employee, there are four approaches I've seen organizations take.

Organization Doesn't Ask

This is sad but true. There are still organizations around the world that simply don't ask employees for feedback or ideas or encourage them to share their opinions. Oftentimes when employees in these types of organizations do speak up, they get squashed by bureaucracy and office politics. I won't mention the specific names of companies here, but with a bit of searching online, it's quite easy to find the organizations out there that simply do not value the opinions of their people. Not coincidentally, these places are also having financial troubles and are poorly ranked and rated online.

Organization Asks but Does Nothing

There are, of course, organizations that do ask for employee feedback and encourage employees to share their opinions, but then they do nothing with them. From the employee's perspective this is pretty much the equivalent of not asking or encouraging feedback and opinions at all. The mentality here is quite simple. Don't ask or encourage employees to share anything with you if aren't prepared to actually do something about it.

Organization Asks and Acknowledges

Next we have organizations who encourage employee feedback and acknowledge when they get it, but they still don't do anything with the information they receive. Instead employees receive a "Thanks for your feedback" e-mail, the kind that you would get when submitting a customer service request to an airline for a poor experience. I see this all the time with various internal surveys, focus groups, or discussions that employees participate in. Of course, it's great to acknowledge the feedback that your employees are giving you, but what's more valuable is actually acting on it.

Organization Asks, Acknowledges, and Acts

This is what is missing from many organizations today: asking, acknowledging, and then acting on the ideas, feedback, and opinions that employees are willing to share with you. And it's not just taking action but also doing so transparently within a reasonable timeline. I'll explore a model for this in a later part of the book.

EMPLOYEES ARE RECOGNIZED FOR THE WORK THAT THEY DO

Recognizing employees for work they do should be a common practice, and there are many ways that this can be done. Sadly, we have spent so much time turning everything we do into a process or a formula that recognizing employees for their hard work doesn't even feel special anymore or even human for that matter. I fly quite a bit and on a recent flight, a United Airlines representative handed me a card when I boarded the plane. I opened the card and it had a message typed on there that said something along the lines of "Thanks for being a loyal flyer" with some person's signature at the bottom. The lady who handed me this card did so while she was announcing, "Now boarding Group 1." This isn't recognition; this is process. It's the organization's way of saying, "For all people who travel X number of miles, hand them this piece of paper." Granted, I'm not an employee at United Airlines, but this is the same feeling many employees get inside of their organizations when they get a $50 gift card for being at the company for three years.

The key distinction here is that just because an organization has a program to recognize employees doesn't mean that they actually feel recognized. This doesn't mean all rewards and recognition programs are bad. Clearly they aren't. I just want to encourage you to think more about the people being recognized and less about the template or the process being used to recognize them. How about a personalized, handwritten note? A special project for them to work on? A round of applause in front of their peers and other leaders? Here are some things to consider. You can look at table 7.2 to see who some of the highest and lowest scoring companies for this variable are.

- Leverage technology but don't forget the humanity.
- Understand what employees care about and how they want to be recognized (ask; don't tell).
- Look at recognition not just from a monetary standpoint but also from an emotional perspective.
- It's okay to have a process and guidelines in place, but remember you're dealing with people, not robots.
- Ask yourself, "Would this make me feel recognized?"

What This Measures
- Employee satisfaction with overall compensation
- Whether employees feel like they are being listened to
- Recognition and feeling valued

TABLE 7.2   Employees Are Recognized for The Work That They Do

Some Highest-Scoring Organizations	Some Lowest-Scoring Organizations
Ultimate Software	Sears
Facebook	HP
Google	Safeway
Hyland Software	CVS Health

What You Can Do

- Spend some time understanding your people; talk them about non-work things.
- Try to move beyond the typical process to focus on the human aspects of making employees feel valued. It's okay to be creative.
- Empower managers to go beyond the typical recognition template to make employees feel good.

LEGITIMATE SENSE OF PURPOSE

It's no surprise that having a sense of purpose is part of creating a CELEBRATED culture. Any engagement, culture, or workplace survey typically has some component that looks at an employee's sense of purpose and for good reason. A sense of purpose helps employees feel connected to the organization they are working for, but it also helps the organization make sure that employees are doing their best work and, most important, that they are doing the work because they want to do it, not because they need to do it. But where does this legitimate sense of purpose come from? Is it something the organization has to create and provide, or is it something that employees have to bring with them? The answer is both.

Employees don't have the luxury of just wandering around waiting for the organization to help them find the meaning of life. That's not quite how this works. There's plenty of due diligence that employees need to do to make sure that they end up working at an organization whose values and purpose matches their own. A big part of creating a sense of purpose comes down to self-awareness: understanding who you are, what you care about, what drives and motivates you, who you want to become, and what impact you want to have. This is not something that any organization can provide for you, and this is the very first step that has to be taken when purpose is discussed in relation to work.

But organizations can certainly help create that sense of purpose, and the most effective organizations that do this focus on two things. They connect the work that employees do back to the reason the organization exists and allow employees to see the direct impact of the work they are doing.

As the story goes, in 1962 President John F. Kennedy was visiting the NASA space center. While taking a tour he noticed a janitor carrying a broom. President Kennedy stopped his tour to say hello. He walked over to the man and said, "Hi, I'm Jack Kennedy. What are you doing?" "Well, Mr. President," the janitor responded, "I'm helping put a man on the moon." The janitor didn't say he was cleaning the floors or emptying trash. He felt like the work he was doing had a much greater impact. If you were to ask employees at your organization this same question, what sort of responses would you get back?

Salesforce.com does a great job of creating a sense of purpose and alignment through something it created called V2MOM, which stands for:

- Vision—what you want to do or achieve
- Values—beliefs that help you pursue that vision
- Methods—actions to get the job done
- Obstacles—challenges you have to overcome to achieve the vision
- Measures—measurable results you aim to achieve

The corporate V2MOM starts at the very top of the organization and then moves down to teams, functions, and even individuals. In fact at Salesforce.com all employees have their own V2MOM, which helps them clearly understand how their involvement and contributions affect the company. All the employees at Salesforce.com can see each other's V2MOMs, which makes this a very transparent process.

Clearly this approach is making a difference at the company because over the years Salesforce.com has won dozens of awards highlighting its workplace practices, including being featured on *Fortune*'s Best Places to Work list for the past five years and *Forbes*'s World's Most Innovative Companies list for the past six years (most recently being ranked second).[5]

Many years ago I used to work at a movie theater behind the concession stand. Actually, I worked at two movie theaters (both large chains). When selling products we were always encouraged to upsell customers to get the larger popcorn and the larger drink (because we all need a trough of popcorn and a gallon of soda). "For just a dollar more you can have a large popcorn and a large drink. Do you want to upgrade?" We did this because we were told to do this, and at the end of each month, the person who upsold the most would get some sort of gift card. Where did the money go? How was it used? What impact did we have on the business by doing this? Did anyone even care? Did customers appreciate this? We didn't know anything except for the fact that we needed to try to get everyone to upgrade. Employees at the movie theater had no idea how what we did affected the company or the customers who came in. The only training that employees were given was about the tactical aspects of how do their jobs, in other words how to ring up a customer, how to make the popcorn, and how to change the soda bag when it ran out. Even though we were selling popcorn in a movie theater, these large chains could have helped create that legitimate sense of purpose. After all, this is where the world came to watch all of their favorite stars. Entertainment happened at the theater! That to me sounds like a compelling story to create purpose.

Let's contrast this same approach with the employees who work the concession stand at the San Diego Zoo, the same nonprofit we met earlier in the technology section of this book. They are also asked to upsell customers and encourage them to walk away with more, just like when I was working at the movie theatre. The difference is that at the San Diego Zoo, the employees know why they are doing this and what the impact is on conservation efforts and on the animals the zoo houses and tries to help. These employees aren't doing it because they get a gift card. They are doing it because they love animals, and they want to help save, rescue, and take care of as many animals as the zoo can. What do they do to make this connection between what employees do and what the impact is?

It starts with the hiring process. To achieve the vision of ending extinction, the zoo must first ignite a passion for wildlife within the daily responsibilities of the employees. This is why one of the factors that the San Diego Zoo looks at is an applicant's roar factor, essentially the passion for wildlife and the spirit to share this passion with guests and colleagues. This goes beyond just hiring someone based on his or her skills or ability to do the job, which is what many movie theater employees and I were hired for. The zoo wants engaging and enthusiastic employees because it believes that every person from the food server to the scientist makes a difference in the wildlife.

Employees get immersed in the mission and vision of the zoo from day one with the new employee orientation called Explore the Roar. This program along with the GRRREAT customer service training program were redesigned at the end of 2015 to include The Call, that is, the strategic initiatives to Unite, Fight, and Ignite. In 2016 the zoo brought in around 1,000 seasonal employees, and every one of them is reminded that they can have a powerful influence on their guests, coworkers, and the public to join in the fight to end extinction. The president and CEO of the San Diego Zoo tells the employees, "Every zoo has lions, tigers, and bears. What they don't have is *you*. It's you who make us world famous!"

In addition to hiring the right people, all the internal communication efforts highlight the topics from The Call, especially the ways the zoo is leading the fight to end extinction. They share conservation and animal welfare stories regularly to make the connection between work and impact. The GRRREAT News e-mail publication is also a regular reminder of the important achievements of employees, as well as compliments from guests and teammates.

All retail employees participate in The Spark training program, which shows employees how their work directly contributes to the achievement of the zoo's vision of ending extinction. The program includes the value and importance of upselling and how that extra revenue contributes toward the vision of the company. Check out the story and the message that these employees receive and experience, taken directly from the San Diego Zoo.

> Close your eyes. Picture your favorite wild animal. Picture it in its native habitat. Raise your hand now, if your animal is in danger due to pollution, poaching, loss of habitat, climate change, or disease. Just about everyone should have their hand raised, as there is no wild species that is not affected by these dangers.
>
> We are all in the right place, as the zoo is leading the fight against the very things that are endangering our favorite species. And through our Uniting Call, we are partnering with outside organizations to make sure that our efforts reach every corner of the planet. Now we just need the funding to make this happen.
>
> Close your eyes, once more. Picture your location. Picture your gift shop, restaurant, cart. Now picture it busy, lots of guests, everywhere. Now, narrow your gaze to just one guest, standing in front of you. This guest is not just a tourist or a member. This unique, special individual is the key to saving our favorite animals. They are the hero and champion for your favorite species. Imagine the impact your guest can make with a purchase, a vision, or a passion that they can carry home and share. Can one inspired person make a difference? Of course! Now broaden your gaze again, see all those other guests in your location. Think of the impact all of them can make, with our help. We can truly make an impact, if we *ignite* these guests to our cause. You can make that impact.
>
> So how do we Ignite our guests? We need to be the Spark.

The *r* in Spark stands for Reach, and the training encourages the following to expand the reach:

1. Offer a *personalized* addition to their transaction
2. Inform them of the value in an upgraded item
3. Direct them to additional experience enhancements

As an employee of the San Diego Zoo, how can you not want to upsell every customer after reading something like that and being immersed in the fight to end extinction? For every extra burger sold, for every drink that is upgraded, or for every toy that people walk away with, the employees at these concessions stands know how that extra money will be used to help the zoo. That's a legitimate sense of purpose.

KPMG is one of the big four professional services firms and employs almost 200,000 people around the world. In 2015 it launched a new purpose statement for the company, which was "Inspire Confidence. Empower Change." Quite an interesting purpose statement for an organization that is typically known for doing auditing, accounting, and consulting work. Still, KPMG realized what many organizations today are figuring out. Words are meaningless without something to back them up. So KPMG embarked on a journey to create and inspire a sense of purpose among its employees. To do this it created stories to show how KPMG affected global historic events, such as managing the Lend-Lease Act, which helped defeat Nazi Germany, and certifying the election of Nelson Mandela in South Africa in 1994. Perhaps most important is that KPMG created stories on an individual employee level. Over 42,000 employees were featured in posters that said things such as "I combat terrorism" or "I help farms grow." These posters featured employees' names and faces along with how KPMG does these various things. The end of each poster stated, "KPMG. You're here for a purpose."

Simply by telling these stories and connecting what employees do to what KPMG stands for, Bruce N. Pfau, partner, Human Capital Strategy and Culture Transformation at KPMG reported that 90 percent of employees saw the higher-purpose initiatives increased people's pride in KPMG, and 76 percent of its employees said their "job had special meaning (and was not just a job)."[6] Not surprisingly, employees whose leaders discussed this higher purpose with them scored considerably higher on all of KPMG's internal metrics than those whose managers did not discuss the higher purpose.

In his book *Give and Take*, Adam Grant shared a great story of how helping people feel a sense of purpose improves productivity. To explore this he looked at paid employees who worked for a university fund-raising center. These employees had the responsibility of calling people up and asking for contributions. As someone who did something similar many years ago, I can absolutely say it feels like a thankless job and it's hard work. Adam found that when these employees were given the chance to actually meet someone who had benefited from their fund-raising efforts and speak with them for a few minutes, over the next month, their weekly fund-raising went up by over 400 percent.[7]

Making these connections and helping employees understand the impact they are having is the best way to help create that sense of purpose. These stories are not unique nor are they rare. A legitimate sense of purpose is the cornerstone of a CELEBRATED culture. You can look at table 7.3 to see who some of the highest and lowest scoring companies for this variable are.

What This Measures

- Connection and commitment to the company
- Organization genuinely cares about employees
- Personal and organizational value alignment

What You Can Do

- Help employees feel like they are a part of your organization's story.
- Connect the work employees do back to the Reason for Being.
- Physically show employees how the work they are doing is affecting customers, the community, or the world.

TABLE 7.3   Legitimate Sense of Purpose

Some Highest-Scoring Organizations	Some Lowest-Scoring Organizations
Facebook	NetApp
St. Jude Children's Research Hospital	W. L. Gore & Associates
Power Home Remodeling	Visa
Ultimate Software	TJX Companies

EMPLOYEES FEEL LIKE THEY'RE PART OF A TEAM

Work is a team sport that relies on multiple people and groups coming together to achieve something. These teams can either be formally structured or be created on an as needed basis. Sometimes these teams comprise individuals in the same geographic location, but in today's globally distributed and connected world, it's far more likely that these teams are spread out all over the world. Today we think of teams in terms of departments, such as marketing, sales, research and development (R&D), HR, and so on. However, teams need to be thought of as groups of people that can be pointed at various problems that need to be solved or opportunities that need to be uncovered. This means that someone in marketing could be a part of an R&D team that is looking to design and develop a new product. Someone in HR could be part of a sales team that is looking to sell consulting services to other organizations. Teams are meant to be dynamic, nimble, and adjustable versus being confined to the common organizational chart. An article written by Susan McDaniel, the president of the American Psychological Association, called "Why Teamwork Surpasses the Individual Approach" stated that "errors in aviation and health care were often linked to traditional hierarchies that shut down communication from anyone but the leader. Teams with diverse membership, flattened hierarchies and rich communication were more likely to have positive outcomes."[8]

Priyanka B. Carr and Gregory M. Walton from Stanford University tested this idea further in five experiments. Participants were asked to solve a puzzle and were told that they could have as much or as little time as they needed. Half of the participants were given hints and cues to suggest that they were a part of a broader group working, and the other half of the participants were not (suggesting they were working independently). Those who felt like they were working on this puzzle as a part of a team worked 48 percent longer than those who didn't. Not only that but participants were also asked to complete a survey after the experiment, and those who felt like they were a part of a team rated the puzzle as being more interesting. According to Walton, "Simply feeling like you're part of a team of people working on a task makes people more motivated as they take on challenges."[9]

Our organizations, and for that matter our educational institutions, haven't done a good job of shifting from focusing on the individual to focusing on the team. In fact many training programs or courses on team building and development are actually designed for individuals to take them, which is a bit paradoxical.

When you join an organization, you want to feel like you belong, like you are a part of something, and like you are around peers. You want to feel like you are a part of a team where you are in this with others and where you know that you can rely on others to have your back. This is why companies like LinkedIn are so explicit in creating a sense of belonging and why Airbnb's mission is to allow people, not just customers, but also employees, to feel like they belong anywhere.

According to Deloitte's "Global Human Capital Trends 2016," this is one of the key priorities and strategic imperatives for organizations around the world. Employees are more empowered than ever, customer expectations are higher, competitors are moving faster, technological change is growing exponentially, and products and services need to be created and pushed out faster. Our organizations are simply not structured to deal with this. One very clear sign of this is the focus on the annual individual employee review. That very concept and practice already signals that employees are being analyzed as individuals, not as team members.

At Facebook all the language used internally is focused on the teams and not on specific individuals. In fact job titles inside the company don't really matter. All the business impact that Facebook sees is brought back down to the team level, and the company is constantly hosting team building events and contests to help drive home this mentality. At Facebook, you are a part of a team.

Employees who don't feel like they are a part of a team will be more reserved, conservative, and less inclined to share their ideas, to think outside the proverbial box, or to go above and beyond expectations to help others. You can look at table 7.4 to see who some of the highest and lowest scoring companies for this variable are.

TABLE 7.4   Employees Feel like They're Part of a Team

Some Highest-Scoring Organizations	Some Lowest-Scoring Organizations
Google	Berkshire Hathaway
Facebook	Perkins Coie
St. Jude Children's Research Hospital	General Dynamics
Power Home Remodeling	Arnold & Porter

What This Measures

- Creating a cohesive and welcoming environment
- Trust
- Psychological safety and feeling like someone has your back
- Communication and collaboration

What You Can Do

- Create teams based on needs and opportunities, not based on organizational charts.
- Reward teams as a whole, not just individual star performers.
- Use social cues to help people feel like they are a part of a team.
- Allow employees to be a part of more than one team.

BELIEVES IN DIVERSITY AND INCLUSION

Every person and talent executive whom I have spoken with in the past few years has always referenced diversity and inclusion as a key focus area. In my previous book, *The Future of Work*, I talked about the importance of having more women in senior management and executive roles, but of course, diversity includes more than just gender. Diversity also means having a diverse group of people based on religion, race, generation, sexual orientation, and more. The Royal Bank of Canada has a great definition of diversity and inclusion: "In simple terms, diversity is the mix of people; inclusion is getting the mix to work well together."[10]

Forbes Insights published a study called "Global Diversity and Inclusion: Fostering Innovation Through a Diverse Workforce," which highlights how diversity affects innovation, productivity, job satisfaction, ability to attract and retain talent, and the like, and being diverse is just the right thing to do and helps contribute to the overall brand image of the organization and hence the overall employee experience. People want to work for organizations that value diverse thought and people of all backgrounds and beliefs. This is also something that millennials and Gen Z employees care about. A study by PricewaterhouseCooper (PwC) called *Millennials at Work: Reshaping the Workplace* found that "millennials value diversity and tend to seek out employers with a strong record on equality and diversity."[11]

Karyn Twaronite is a partner and the global diversity and inclusiveness officer at EY, a multinational professional services firm with over 200,000 employees around the world. In an hourlong discussion I had with her, I asked her what she does, and her response perfectly explains what diversity and inclusiveness is all about. She said, "My role is about our firm appreciating the unique differences and talents of all our people in the 150+ countries [where they operate] and then allowing our teams to best leverage those collective differences so that they can be higher-performing teams, provide the best client service, innovate, and deliver better solutions." Karyn also shared with me that diversity and inclusiveness is not just about gender, religion, and sexual orientation—but it also includes diversity of beliefs, experience, technical expertise, and pretty much anything else that makes people different. Karyn and her team at EY also tie their diversity and inclusiveness efforts to real business impact. As a result they have seen lower turnover, higher retention, higher revenue growth and gross margin, greater team collaboration, and increased brand favorability.

Kaiser Permanente is a healthcare provider with almost 200,000 employees. *DiversityInc* recently ranked it as the number one company for diversity, which is a tremendous achievement. At Kaiser diversity is embedded into every aspect of how the organization operates internally and with suppliers and how it interacts with customers. In fact the chairman and CEO of Kaiser Permanente, Bernard J. Tyson, personally signs off on executive compensation tied to diversity, diversity metrics, and progress, goals, and achievements for supplier diversity. Looking at the Kaiser Glassdoor rankings, it's also quite apparent that this focus on diversity is not only noticed by employees but also extremely appreciated.

Sodexo is a French food services and facilities management company with over 400,000 employees around the world that also has a strong diversity and inclusion effort going on. *DiversityInc* ranked it the number six company for diversity.[12] At Sodexo 25 percent of the executive team's bonus is tied to how well they perform on their diversity scorecard. For management the percentage is 10 to 15 percent.[13] Sodexo credits its diversity and inclusion programs with increasing overall employee happiness and satisfaction as well as expanding its business development opportunities.

The Sodexo diversity and inclusion effort is based on four things:

1. Connection to the business—Build the value of the brand, attract and retain the best people, drive innovation and productivity, grow new business, and improve customer service
2. Leadership commitment—All executives at Sodexo are expected to show their commitment to diversity and inclusion through their words and actions
3. Top down, bottom up, and middle out deployment strategy—Grassroots efforts, executive role modeling, and the cross market diversity council led by midlevel managers
4. Accountability and measurement—Metrics such as the diversity index, which influences pay (discussed earlier)

These are just a few examples of organizations that believe in diversity and inclusion, which makes it easier for them to attract and retain the best and brightest talent in the world. You can look at table 7.5 to see who some of the highest and lowest scoring companies for this variable are.

What This Measures
- Creating an open and welcoming organization
- Respect and appreciation for all employees (and people in general)
- Psychological safety

TABLE 7.5   Believes in Diversity and Inclusion

Some Highest-Scoring Organizations	Some Lowest-Scoring Organizations
Apple	Berkshire Hathaway
Salesforce.com	Perkins Coie
PwC	General Dynamics
American Express	Arnold & Porter

What You Can Do

- Define what diversity and inclusion means to your organization and what it looks like.
- Tie the program to something meaningful, such as executive and management compensation.
- Make it public for the world to see.

REFERRALS COME FROM EMPLOYEES

In the realm of customer experience, there is something called the Net Promoter Score (NPS), which is used to measure customer loyalty by asking a very simple question: "How likely is it that you would recommend our company/product/service to a friend or colleague?" Many organizations have adopted a similar approach with respect to measuring employee loyalty with an eNPS score (the *e* stands for employee). The question is almost identical but instead of focusing on the customers, it asks, "On a scale of zero to 10, how likely is it you would recommend this company as a place to work?" These questions are fine to ask, but I have found that organizations that create truly great employee experiences actually see a high referral rate. That is, employees like working there so much that they tell others to apply.

Many organizations around the world have referral programs where they offer financial incentives and rewards for employees who refer others to work there. Referral programs have been quite popular as of late, thanks to social media and our ability to quickly build networks that organizations would love to tap into for prospective candidates. Although the cause is noble, it misses the whole point of why people refer others for anything. If you go eat at a restaurant and the service and food are terrible, would you refer your friends to eat there if the restaurant gave you $50? Probably not. What if you had this same experience with a babysitter, house cleaner, mechanic, or hotel? Again, chances are that if you don't have a good experience with something, you won't refer your friends or family members to that establishment, even if you get a financial reward. So why do we think that this rule doesn't apply inside of our organizations? It absolutely does. Employees won't refer other people to work at your organization just because you promise them a financial reward. Perhaps more important, would you even want employees to refer their friends just because they are getting a cash reward? When the only incentive is money, the outcome will always be transactional, which is not a good way to think about your people. The financial reward acts as an incentive only if the employees genuinely have a good experience working there to begin with.

Google figured this out quickly. Originally it set its employee referral bonus program at $2,000, meaning an employee would get $2,000 for referring someone who got hired. It wanted to increase employee referrals, so it did what any company would do: doubled the bonus to $4,000! This approach proved unsuccessful. According to Laszlo Bock, Google's former senior vice president of people operations (who still advises the company), "It turned out that nobody was meaningfully motivated by the referral bonus. . . . People [who referred other employees] actually loved their work experience and wanted other people to share it. Only rarely did people mention the referral bonus." So what was Google's solution? Simple, it just made it easier for employees to refer others by nudging them with relevant openings and hosting "Sourcing Jams."[14]

People refer others to work at your organization when the employee experience is great. That's why this is a useful question to ask and a metric to look at. According to a Facebook executive I spoke with, their employee referral rate is between 30 and 50 percent, which is quite astonishing but not surprising, considering it scored higher than any other organization on the Employee Experience Index, which shows

TABLE 7.6   Referrals Come from Employees

Some Highest-Scoring Organizations	Some Lowest-Scoring Organizations
Facebook	Express Scripts
Salesforce.com	AIG
Accenture	Sears
Google	Kroger

that people truly want to work there. We also have to remember that the employee referral door swings both ways. Sometimes employees will refer their network to work at your organization, but sometimes they will send warning signs to anyone and everyone they know who might be applying to work there. You can look at table 7.6 to see who some of the highest and lowest scoring companies for this variable are.

What This Measures

- Whether employees genuinely like working for the organization
- Loyalty and commitment to the organization

What You Can Do

- Shift away from asking whether employees *would* refer their friends to work there to *do* they actually do so.
- Have a goal for what you want your employee referral rate to be and track it.
- Create programs that don't focus on just financial incentives for employees. Otherwise the referrals will occur for the wrong reasons.

ABILITY TO LEARN NEW THINGS AND GIVEN THE RESOURCES TO DO SO AND ADVANCE

Albert Einstein famously said, "Once you stop learning, you start dying." As I mentioned earlier, humans are naturally curious and inquisitive. When we learn we grow, both as individuals and as employees. So what happens when you feel like you are in a position where you have nothing left to learn and nowhere to grow? At that point you're really just a body inside the organization until you can (and eventually will) find something better. You become someone who is just there for a paycheck, and your experience is negatively affected to the point where you no longer even want to be a part of that organization. Randstad, a placement agency with around 30,000 employees around the world, recently surveyed about 11,000 U.S. workers and found that the number one reason people leave their jobs is lack of career path.[15]

One of the key things in a career path is the phrase "given the resources to do so." This means that the organization actually gives employees whatever resources they need to grow or advance. This could be mentoring programs, cash to take courses online, internal training sessions, employee groups, guest speakers, or a whole range of other things. Employees need to feel like when they want to grow, they can.

Let's break this attribute down into the individual components because although they are all related, learning and development and advancement are not the same.

Learning and Development

Although this can encompass quite a lot of things, at its heart, learning and development is designed to make sure that employees never stop learning and adapting to the changing world. New skills, strategies, techniques, processes, attitudes, values, and behaviors are all part of learning and development. A great example can be found in HR. Traditional HR is going through an amazing transformation today. Instead of simply focusing on hiring, firing, rules, and procedures, HR is now having to explore experience, new technologies, engagement, multiple generations, organizational design, and much more. Ideally, an organization would offer learning and development programs to help HR professionals adapt to these changes. The same is true for any other employee in any function. Things change and we need to be able to adapt. Learning and development helps make sure that we continue to grow as individuals. This also keeps us from getting bored, opens up new challenges and opportunities, helps us feel more successful, and adds more color to our professional and our personal lives. Learning is also more than just something we want. It's a biological imperative that keeps our brains and thus our bodies healthy.

Qlik is a business intelligence–visualization software company with over 2,500 employees. Lisa Carraway, director, internal communications, shared some of the fun and interesting things it is doing. When conducting its internal employee survey, it found that team members were not only seeking more opportunities for development (beyond just classes or programs) but also time to actually take advantage of new offerings. As part of its investment in learning and development, it launched the global 24-For-U program in the first quarter of 2016 for all Qlik team members to encourage nontraditional learning and development experiences. This program provides an additional day off per year for education—whether it benefits personally or professionally—including training programs, time with a subject matter expert, shadowing someone for the day, and so on. Everyone is encouraged to keep 24-For-U in mind when creating his or her annual individual development plans. From Qlik's perspective, if a person is learning and growing, he or she is going to be happier and more engaged. Employees have used this new initiative in some pretty creative and engaging ways.

A Qlik team member in the Radnor, PA, office is currently enrolled in an MBA program and used his 24-For-U day during his immersion program in Buenos Aires, Argentina. He shared that his 24-For-U day included meeting the mayor of Pilar (a province in Buenos Aires) in the morning, attending an afternoon working session on doing business in Argentina by PwC's head of strategy, meeting with the managing partner of Cleary Gottlieb to discuss Argentine financial markets in the evening, and ending the day by attending a Dinner & Tango Show.

Another team member combined his 24-For-U day with his corporate social responsibility day and vacation time to travel to an orphanage in Peru. Together with two Qlik colleagues, he helped install a computer lab in the orphanage's learning center. In this case, the benefit of 24-For-U goes far beyond the development the Qlik team experienced and extends to the children at the orphanage. The technology will be key to improving their lives by enhancing communications and technical skills and preparing them for their future of work. Other team members supported the cause with donations, and Qlik promptly doubled those donations.

An analyst in the Vancouver office is currently preparing for a financial and valuation modeling boot camp that will provide her with financial skills to complement her market and competitive intelligence expertise. This will help her grow in her current position. She used her 24-For-U day to work on the accounting prerequisites with an online preparation program called Wall Street Prep.

Lisa used her 24-For-U day to learn more about the documentary filmmaking process to support a veterans' program called Grand Canyon Warriors—an annual trip on the Colorado River to help wounded vets with their recovery. She thought a short documentary would be a great way to raise awareness and funds. However, she had worked only on corporate videos and had no experience or budget to create a film. So, she took an online course on how to draft a film treatment and met with corporate video contacts for their counsel. As an executive producer Lisa developed communications and leadership skills and applied professional experience to a charitable effort. Most important, she was able to contribute to the Grand Canyon Warriors in a much greater way than she could ever have imagined—this was priceless! Her team is in the middle stages of production but is very much looking forward to having this film contribute to making a difference in the lives of wounded veterans.

Qlik is a great example of an organization that takes a more unconventional approach toward learning and development. Its 24-For-U initiative not only helps develop team members but also does so in an engaging way that makes people actually want to take advantage of the effort. So many organizations struggle with getting employees to actually participate in development programs. Why not try something unique like Qlik did?

Perhaps no other organization in the world takes learning as seriously as Accenture, a global professional services company with over 350,000 employees around the world. I spoke with both its chief learning officer, Rahul Varma, and its chief leadership and HR officer, Ellyn Shook. Last year alone Accenture spent upwards of $841 million dollars on learning, which is one of the world's largest budgets devoted to this category. It is currently on the path to create over 100 digital employee classrooms at its various locations around the world. Its approach is instead of taking learners to great learning, it should be taking great learning to its learners. This means you can be anywhere in the world and get access to a top-notch learning infrastructure.

Accenture has six pillars that are a part of its learning delivery strategy, which are regional, local, virtual, on demand, on the job, and communities. These are essentially the six ways that employees can leverage learning. This plethora of options means that employees can teach others, access face-to-face instruction, join virtual classrooms, or even get access to content such as HarvardX, which are free online courses Harvard University offers.

Advancement

This is not the same thing as learning and development, although organizations oftentimes place them in the same bucket. Advancement specifically refers to the forward motion in an individual's career, typically signified with a promotion and a pay raise. If you start as an associate and then get promoted to manager, then you have experienced advancement. According to a study done by EY (a 200,000-person global professional services firm) called *Global Generations: A Global Study on Work-Life Challenges across Generations*, one of the top reasons why people quit their jobs is a lack of advancement opportunities. This should come as no surprise, though, because forward motion signifies progress.

These are the conventional definitions of what learning and development and advancement are, but here's where things get a bit tricky. Employees have their own perspective on what these things actually mean. In other words, for some employees who say they want advancement, really what they are talking about is learning new things, gaining more responsibility, and expanding their skill set. Sometimes they don't even care about money or a promotion. Other times employees who say they want advancement are specifically talking about a pay raise and a promotion. They want more money and a more senior title. This is why it's so crucial to have the conversations with employees about what they are actually looking for. You may uncover that one of the reasons why employees want more senior job titles is so that their resumes look good for future employers. These employees may care less about what their title is in their current role, but they want others to know that they have been growing and advancing. Understanding the motives behind why employees are asking for or wanting certain things will make it much easier for you to give it to them. This is one of the reasons why T-Mobile has focused so much on creating a culture of promoting within and has an internal promotion rate of 90 percent, which is unheard of in any industry or for any company.[16]

This also means that you can start to get creative. You may work at an organization that has no job titles or perhaps has just a few job titles to help keep the organization structure relatively flat. Well in that type of scenario, suppose an employee leaves the company, and the prospective employer says, "Hmm, you've been at this company for five years with the same job title. What's up with that?" What can you do? You can give employees job titles that they can use externally on their resumes or social media profiles. Whether you use existing job titles, create new ones, eliminate them altogether, or just allow employees to use job titles externally, the point is that employees want to feel like they are both learning new things and moving up in the company.

I've told this story in my previous book, *The Future of Work*, but one of the reasons why I left the business world to go off on my own was because of bad experiences I had working for other people. One experience in particular really helped push me toward leaving the corporate world. I graduated from college with honors and earned a dual BA in business management economics and psychology. After the organization I interviewed for promised me that I'd be doing all sorts of fun and exciting work, I was stuck doing data entry, cold calling, and PowerPoint presentations. The last straw for me was when an executive came out of his office, handed me a $10 bill, and asked me to go him coffee. Clearly I was stuck at an organization where I couldn't advance or learn anything new. Years have gone by since that happened, and now here you are, reading this book. I suppose I should thank that executive for making me get him coffee. You can look at table 7.7 to see who some of the highest and lowest scoring companies for this variable are.

TABLE 7.7 Ability to Learn New Things and Given the Resources to Do So and Advance

Some Highest-Scoring Organizations	Some Lowest-Scoring Organizations
Apple	Mercedes-Benz USA
Google	Safeway
LinkedIn	INTL FCStone
Kimpton Hotels & Restaurants	L. L. Bean

What This Measures

- Career progression and personal growth ability and opportunities
- Understanding of employee motives internally and externally
- Investment in people

What You Can Do

- Separate the discussions about learning and development and advancement.
- Determine the true motives of employees. Are they interested in growth or just having more money and a fancier title?

TREATS EMPLOYEES FAIRLY

Let's say a new promotion comes up at your organization that you are clearly qualified and ready for, but instead your manager gives the promotion to someone who used to be his or her college roommate (and because of it). Clearly that's not a fair situation and would cause anyone to be quite upset. Fairness means free from bias, dishonesty, or injustice. This isn't an easy thing to do because as humans we all have subjective ways of perceiving people, things, and situations. If an organization is biased, dishonest, and plagued with injustice, then why on earth would anyone want to work there? But treating employees fairly doesn't mean treating everyone the same.

Let's say someone on the marketing team leaked confidential information. You don't fire the entire marketing team. Similarly if someone in sales brought in a big client, you probably won't reward or recognize the entire sales team. Treating everyone the same is a great approach for making employees feel like cogs. After all, these employees have different jobs, work preferences, tasks they are working on, skills and abilities, and personalities. Do you treat all your friends the same? What about your kids? If you have a 13-year-old daughter and a 22-year-old son, do they both have the same curfew, allowance, and rules they have to follow? I'm guessing the answer is no. Still, it doesn't mean that you can't treat your kids, and employees, fairly.

Fairness is a tricky animal because as humans we are inherently flawed, and whether we realize it or not, we aren't always fair to one another. We've all been in situations in our personal lives where we weren't treated fairly. These are not typically pleasant experiences. If employees report that they are being treated unfairly, then clearly this not only becomes an employee experience issue but also becomes, potentially, a legal issue.

It's very easy for us to identify when we are being treated unfairly, but it's much harder for us to identify the specific things that are required for everyone to be treated fairly. Among other things, treating employees fairly means:

- Knowing them as people, not just as job functions
- Understanding personal circumstances and situations
- Listening to all employees
- Giving everyone a fair and honest opportunity without stacking the deck
- Being empathetic and when needed sympathetic
- Acting like a human and treating other employees like grown-ups

This is why many organizations today are offering training in the areas of bias detection, empathy, and emotional intelligence. The goal is to help all employees feel like they are treated fairly. You can look at table 7.8 to see who some of the highest and lowest scoring companies for this variable are.

TABLE 7.8   Treats Employees Fairly

Some Highest-Scoring Organizations	Some Lowest-Scoring Organizations
Ultimate Software	Visa
Facebook	Mondelēz International
Veterans United Home Loans	Ingram Micro
Airbnb	DuPont

What This Measures

- How employees are treated
- Balanced and flexible approach to employee relationships

What You Can Do

- Communicate your practices of being fair but not homogenous.
- Try to eliminate biases when and where you can.

EXECUTIVES AND MANAGERS ARE COACHES AND MENTORS

For the longest time we have had this collective assumption inside of our organizations that executives and managers sit at the very top of the organizational pyramid and everyone else sits below them. Those at the top typically have all the power and all the information, and everyone else below them simply do what they are told. In this type of organization the managers and the executives are the supreme rulers, and everyone else is just there to do their job. This assumption was well justified because the entire field of management and the existence of managers was created to enforce the status quo. The whole point of management and managers was to make sure that people fell in line.

Thankfully this way of thinking is being challenged at every company I have come across and for good reason. Senior leaders play a big role in shaping and designing employee experiences, so in organizations where managers act like rulers and dictators, the employee experience suffers tremendously. According to Gallup, managers account for a 70 percent variance in employee engagement (which is the outcome of employee experience).[17]

Instead, managers and executives must see themselves not at the top of the proverbial company pyramid, where everyone climbs to them, but at the bottom of the pyramid, where they push everyone else up. In fact I'm a firm believer that one of the measures of success for managers should be how many people and how often they help make other people more successful than themselves. This was something that was discussed at length in a great book called *Superbosses* by Sydney Finkelstein. Not coincidentally at Google, being a good coach is also the number one behavior that makes a great manager. I should also point out that Google discovered this after doing extensive research and analysis which looked at employee surveys, exit interviews, performance and satisfaction data, and turnover. Then they ran several internal tests and experiments.

When you hire a trainer at the gym, his or her responsibility is to help get you in shape. Trainers give you meals plans and workouts, check in with you on the phone, encourage you, and push you to achieve their goals. They also get to know you as an individual and customize training programs that meet your needs. In other words, their job is to help make you successful. Managers are the modern-day organizational fitness trainers.

Chances are you've heard the saying that employees don't leave organizations (or jobs); they leave managers. One of the best ways to keep that from happening is by embracing the coach and mentor mentality. Help employees succeed and if you can, help them become more successful than you! When Facebook did an internal study to find which behaviors the best managers exhibit, "they care about their team members" was number one on the list.[18] You can look at table 7.9 to see who some of the highest and lowest scoring companies for this variable are.

What This Measures
- Managers invested in the success of employees
- Having the right managers in place

**TABLE 7.9   Executives and Managers
Are Coaches and Mentors**

Some Highest-Scoring Organizations	Some Lowest-Scoring Organizations
Ultimate Software	Tesla
Hilti	Visa
Best Buy	HP
Cardinal Health	Berkshire Hathaway

What You Can Do

- Educate and train managers to think of themselves like coaches and mentors.
- Explore the success rate of the people whom managers oversee to determine which managers help others succeed the most.

DEDICATED TO EMPLOYEE HEALTH AND WELLNESS

A few years ago when I would ask executives whether they had employee health and wellness programs, they would say, "Absolutely, we pay for their gym memberships and they get healthy snacks." We've come a long way since assuming health and wellness is about food and muscles. Today health and wellness means focusing on the mind and the body. According to the American Institute of Stress, our jobs are by far the leading cause of stress in our lives, but this isn't just true in the United States. This is common in various regions around the world. We work longer hours, we're more connected, our attention spans are shorter, and we just can't seem to find the time in the day to do everything we need to get done. Oftentimes this means we skimp out on the time we need to keep ourselves healthy. We don't have time to eat breakfast, so we grab a giant caramel mocha and an egg sandwich from McDonald's; we'd love to work out, but we have that big presentation that's due, so we have to skip the gym; and we can't relax and have time to ourselves after work because we keep checking our e-mail every 5 seconds. Then, of course, we have family and all sorts of other things going on in our personal lives that we need to deal with. The point is we live in a new world where things move faster and we're always connected.

Workplace stress can lead to all sorts of unhealthy habits and problems that affect our bodies. Weight gain, poor eating habits, heart problems, trouble sleeping, depression, and anxiety are just a few of the common things that we can experience because of workplace stress. This keeps us from doing and being our best at work and at home. Organizations around the world are acknowledging this shift and are doing all sorts of things to help keep employees' minds and bodies healthy. Health and education training programs, healthy snacks and meals, gym memberships, access to nutritionists, team and company fitness contests, nap rooms, wearable fitness devices to track activity, and walking meetings are just some of the things that are being implemented at organizations around the world. Then we have to focus on the mind, which includes stress workshops, financial planning advisors to help with saving for retirement and college tuition, yoga and meditation classes, and the like.

The forward-thinking organizations understand that part of their responsibility isn't just providing a job for their employees. It's also looking after them and taking care of them. Although health and wellness programs are typically experienced while employees are at work, their impact are oftentimes felt at home as well. Employees who feel taken care of will be more relaxed, will have more energy to give their friends and family members, will feel better about themselves, and in general will lead a happier life. There are plenty of benefits for organizations as well, such as reduced absenteeism and healthcare costs, higher employee morale, and lower employee turnover.

Still, health and wellness doesn't mean offering short-term solutions to long-term employee needs. It means having an organizational commitment to looking after employees. An article published the *Harvard Business Review* by Hector De La Torre and Ron Goetzel, PhD called "How to Design a Corporate Wellness Plan That Actually Works" stated that "one-time events masquerading as health promotion programs—that is, activities not integrated into a comprehensive workplace health promotion strategy—are likely to fail."[19]

Marriott International is a global hospitality company with around 200,000 employees around the world, and it truly believes in employee health and wellness. In fact its global chief human resources officer, David Rodriguez, believes its wellness program helped save his life. He was diagnosed with leukemia and through its TakeCare program was able to successfully make it through chemotherapy while learning new habits that helped put him in a better physical and mental place. In 2016 (and onward) health and well-being became something that Marriott really wanted to push globally, so this became a unified goal that started at the top with the CEO of Marriott International and was spread to all of his direct reports, which includes every president across every geography. All of these executives were tasked with helping employees learn about the various programs and take advantage of them. This included everything from physical fitness classes to online courses, to financial planning assistance, to getting involved with local community efforts. In turn they see employees become more committed to the company and what it stands for. You can look at table 7.10 to see who some of the highest and lowest scoring companies for this variable are.

What This Measures

- Commitment to overall employee well-being
- Taking care of employees

What You Can Do

- Offer programs for health and wellness that employees are craving.
- Think of health and wellness beyond snacks and gyms.
- Consistently evaluate and update your programs.

HOW ORGANIZATIONS SCORED

The maximum number of points that an organization could have received for each of the above variables was 7 for a total of 70 possible points. Out the 10 variables here, the one with the lowest average (4.5/7) was "Employees feel their managers are coaches and mentors." This is not surprising

TABLE 7.10 Dedicated to Employee Health and Wellness

Some Highest-Scoring Organizations	Some Lowest-Scoring Organizations
LinkedIn	Tesla
Airbnb	Visa
Adobe	David Weekley Homes
Starbucks	Berkshire Hathaway

because the traditional concepts of management and the manager are exact antonyms of "coaches and mentors." Shifting the traditional mentality of management is a major struggle for most organizations. There were two variables that tied for having the highest average with a score of 5.4/7. The first is "Employees feel that the organization they work for is diverse and inclusive," and the second is "Generally speaking, the company has a strong positive brand perception."

On average, the 252 organizations I analyzed scored a 5.1 for each question, or 51/70 for the cultural environment. This comes to 73 percent of the maximum that an organization can get. Again, if this were the University of Employee Experience, then collectively these organizations would get a C for their cultural environment grade.

For many organizations around the world, culture continues to be the elusive beast that they have yet to capture and tame. As you can see culture clearly has the largest impact on employee experience, and it's the most challenging to execute on. This is because unlike physical space and technology, which oftentimes have specific deliverables and actual things that are created and developed, culture deals with more of the human side of things, which oftentimes can't be translated into a deliverable. It's the equivalent of following steps to bake a cake or put together furniture versus following steps to create a healthy marriage. As anyone who has been in a relationship knows, you can't just follow a blueprint or a template to get the perfect relationship. Still, there are plenty of organizations around the world that have done an excellent job of creating a culture worth celebrating—and others that haven't.

TABLE 7.11   The Cultural Environment

Some Highest-Scoring Organizations	Some Lowest-Scoring Organizations
Ultimate Software	Sears
Google	Visa
Facebook	Safeway
Apple	World Fuel Services

Although there are some organizations around the world that are doing an excellent job of investing in employee experiences, the collective average of all the companies I analyzed is far below where we deserve for it to be. When it comes to the cultural environment, you can look at table 7.11 to see who some of the highest and lowest scoring companies are.

When looking at these 17 variables, it's also important to look at what these variables actually measure. For example, when your organization's values are physically reflected, this doesn't just mean you are living your values, but this also measures honesty, integrity, and a commitment to your people. When you give all of your employees access to consumer grade technology, this doesn't just mean you're doing it to be nice or cool. This measures your commitment to empowering your people and driving innovation and collaboration. If employees feel like they are a part of a team, this doesn't just mean employees work well together. This measures trust, psychological safety, and communication and collaboration. The point is not just to focus on the first layer of what these environments and variables actually are, but also to focus on what these things measure. In other words, what does it mean when you have an organization where employees are coaches and mentors? What does it mean when employees have access to multiple workspace options? What does it mean when your organization has a strong diversity and inclusion program?

When you look at employee experience in terms of "What does this mean?" then you will realize the deeper significance of what needs to be done and why.

NOTES

1. Abbot, Lydia, Ryan Batty, and Stephanie Bevegni. *Global Recruiting Trends 2016*. LinkedIn. 2015. https://business.linkedin.com/content/dam/business/talent-solutions/global/en_us/c/pdfs/GRT16_GlobalRecruiting_100815.pdf.
2. Burgess, Wade. "Research Shows Exactly How Much Having a Bad Employer Brand Will Cost You." *LinkedIn Talent Blog*, March 30, 2016. https://business.linkedin.com/talent-solutions/blog/employer-brand/2016/research-shows-exactly-how-much-having-a-bad-employer-brand-will-cost-you.
3. Society for Human Resources Management. *2016 Employee Job Satisfaction and Engagement: Revitalizing a Changing Workforce*. April 2016. https://www.shrm.org/hr-today/trends-and-forecasting/research-and-surveys/Documents/2016-Employee-Job-Satisfaction-and-Engagement-Report.pdf.
4. Indeed Hiring Lab. "The Indeed Job Happiness Index 2016: Ranking the World for Employee Satisfaction." 2016. http://blog.indeed.com/hiring-lab/indeed-job-happiness-index-2016/.
5. "The World's Most Innovative Companies." *Forbes*. 2016. http://www.forbes.com/innovative-companies/#27fee7c1f172.
6. Pfau, Bruce N. "How an Accounting Firm Convinced Its Employees They Could Change the World." *Harvard Business Review*, October 6, 2015. https://hbr.org/2015/10/how-an-accounting-firm-convinced-its-employees-they-could-change-the-world?webSyncID=4256300c-db57-6a2c-20ce-68d4572ec006&sessionGUID=444ae91b-6b9b-066b-a3e0-554d67e03b61.
7. Grant, Adam. *Give and Take: Why Helping Others Drives Our Success*. New York: Penguin Books, 2014.
8. McDaniel, Susan H. "Why Teamwork Surpasses the Individual Approach." *Monitor on Psychology* 47, no. 5 (May 2016): 5.
9. Association for Psychological Science. "Just Feeling Like Part of a Team Increases Motivation on Challenging Tasks." February 24, 2015. http://www.psychologicalscience.org/news/minds-business/just-feeling-like-part-of-a-team-increases-motivation-on-challenging-tasks.html#.WFRZYH25LVI.
10. Royal Bank of Canada. "What Is Diversity & Inclusion?" Accessed December 16, 2016. http://www.rbc.com/diversity/what-is-diversity.html.
11. PricewaterhouseCooper. *Millennials at Work: Reshaping the Workplace*. 2011. https://www.pwc.com/m1/en/services/consulting/documents/millennials-at-work.pdf.
12. "The 2016 DiversityInc Top 50 Companies for Diversity." *DiversityInc*. 2016. http://www.diversityinc.com/the-diversityinc-top-50-companies-for-diversity-2016/.
13. Silva, Betsy. "Diversity & Inclusion: A Strategic Imperative: *The Sodexo Story*." Lecture at Inclusion Change Management Conference, Cleveland, OH, August 17, 2011.
14. Bock, Laszlo. *Work Rules! Insights from Inside Google That Will Transform How You Live and Lead*. New York: Grand Central, 2015.

15. Randstad. "Randstad Survey Reveals More Employees Leave Jobs for Career Growth Than Money." Accessed December 16, 2016. https://www.randstadusa .com/about/news/randstad-survey-reveals-more-employees-leave-jobs-for-career-growth-than-money/.
16. Wireless Vision. "Why WV Is the Place to Be." Accessed December 16, 2016. http://www.wirelessvision.com/careers/.
17. Beck, Randall, and Jim Harter. "Managers Account for 70% of Variance in Employee Engagement." Gallup. April 21, 2015. http://www.gallup.com/businessjournal/182792/managers-account-variance-employee-engagement.aspx.
18. Feloni, Richard. "Facebook's HR Chief Conducted a Company-Wide Study to Find Its Best Managers — and 7 Behaviors Stood Out." Business Insider. January 27, 2016. http://www.businessinsider.com/facebook-best-managers-exhibit-these-7-behaviors-2016-1.
19. De La Torre, Hector, and Ron Goetzel. "How to Design a Corporate Wellness Plan That Actually Works." *Harvard Business Review*, March 31, 2016. https://hbr.org/2016/03/how-to-design-a-corporate-wellness-plan-that-actually-works.

CHAPTER 8

The Employee Experience Equation

The Reason for Being guides how the organization acts when it comes to creating employee experiences. To better visualize the 17 variables that create COOL spaces, ACE technology, and a CELEBRATED culture, I created something called the employee experience equation which you can see in figure 8.1. The goal is to show that all three of these environments are required to create the overall employee experience and the more of the environments you can execute on, the better that experience is going to be.

The original version of this concept had + signs instead of × signs, but the more I started to dig into these environments, the more I realized how much of a dramatic impact they had on one another. This led me to understand that although culture, technology, and the physical environment are very distinct from one another, they each help empower and support the other. For example, one of the attributes of the physical environment is flexibility, yet flexibility is not possible without having the right technologies in place. One of the attributes of the cultural environment is allowing employees to learn and grow. Again this is not possible without having the right technologies in place to allow learning and education at scale in a modern way. We can see in these examples that although technology is its own entity, it also has an impact on the physical and the cultural environments. This same exercise can be done with any

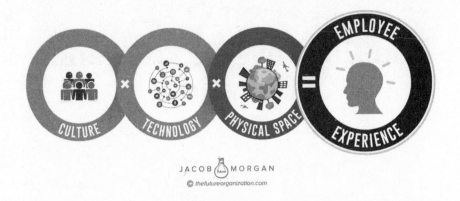

FIGURE 8.1   The Employee Experience Equation

of the three environments. As a result the employee experience equation isn't so much a linear addition as it is an exponential evolution. Organizations that focus on all three of these environments will see a dramatically larger impact when compared with organizations that focus on just one or even two of the environments.

No single environment can get to its maximum potential without having the support of the other two. This is one of the reasons why so many organizations around the world are struggling with not only improving employee engagement but also justifying the investments required. They are stuck focusing on just a small part of the big picture, and even that small part isn't being executed on well.

Thinking of the overall employee experience in this type of equation helps organizations realize that all three environments are crucial and have a much greater impact than the sum of their individual parts. This will become quite clear when you get to the Chapter 11 which focuses on the business value of employee experience.

PART III
Why Invest in Employee Experience?

Thus far we have looked at the Reason for Being along with the three employee experience environments and the attributes that create them, which are COOL physical spaces, ACE technology, and a CELEBRATED culture. We also looked at what these attributes are, why they are important, and some quick tips for things you can do to implement them. The remainder of this book will explore how and what organizations can do to actually go about designing employee experiences that take all of these environments and variables into consideration. To do that we need to understand a few things:

- What does the employee experience methodology look like?
- Who owns the employee experience?
- What does a team that's responsible for employee experience look like?
- What role do employees play in actually designing their own experiences?
- How do we scale employee experiences?

In this part of the book, I will do my best to answer all of these questions.

CHAPTER 9

The Nine Types of Organizations

Organizations fall along different levels of maturity or focus when it comes to designing employee experiences. As my team and I spent more time going through the data, we noticed that a wide range of organizational categories emerged. When I first developed this concept, I had the simple idea of creating four types or organizational categories: those that were great at all three employee experience environments or those that were great two out of the three environments (there are three options here). Unfortunately things weren't so simple. Looking at the data I noticed that some companies scored poorly in all areas, others scored well in all three but not great, and then other organizations really excelled in one environment but ranked poor in the other two. All of these various combinations led me to expand this to a much larger category of organizations.

Based on these attributes there are nine types of organizations that I have identified:

1. inExperienced
2. Technologically emergent
3. Physically emergent
4. Culturally emergent
5. Engaged

6. Empowered
7. Enabled
8. preExperiential
9. Experiential

As you read this you can determine where your organization falls along the spectrum, or better yet, you can actually measure your own Employee Experience Score based on the attributes discussed earlier.

INEXPERIENCED

The first type of organization is one that isn't actively investing in any of the three employee experience environments. InExperienced companies simply exist for the sake of existing. They try to make as much money as possible, and they operate the same way today as they did in the 1990s and 1980s (or earlier). You won't find many young employees at an inExperienced organization, and if you do, they won't be there very long. Hierarchies are the default structure, management operates based on fear and command and control, technologies are all outdated, and the offices are massive cubicle farms. These organizations rarely have a Reason for Being and instead have a standard mission statement, which talks about how they want to be market leaders. It's not surprising that these organizations have the greatest challenges with attracting and retaining talent, driving innovation, communication and collaboration, organizational design, and pretty much anything else that affects the people who work there. These are not very desirable places to work, and thanks to the use of social media tools, current and prospective employees are very much aware that this is the case. Although these types of companies also have the furthest to travel, they are also the ones who can reap the greatest rewards from their journey, provided they are able to get moving. Many companies, especially older ones, start out as being inExperienced. Examples of organizations in this category include Safeway, Caterpillar, Sears, and even the innovative Tesla.

EMERGING

Organizations that focus on just one out of the three environments are known as emerging organizations. They are on their way to designing employee experience hence their name. There are a few subcategories of emerging organizations, which are:

- Physically emerging
- Technologically emerging
- Culturally emerging

Physically emerging organizations typically spend all of their time and resources on designing beautiful places to work, sometimes to the point of extravagance, but this doesn't always have to be the case. You might see slides that employees use to get down to the ground level from upper floors, tons of amazing free food, expensive lighting fixtures, designer office furniture, and pretty much anything else that makes the office space look like it's too nice to sit in. I want to stress that this isn't a bad thing if the organization also takes into account the other two employee experience environments. After all, organizations such as Facebook, LinkedIn, Google, and Salesforce.com all have beautiful office spaces, but they also do an amazing job of investing in culture and technology. Organizations that purely focus on aesthetics will eventually find that the beauty of the physical space starts to fade as employees are faced with the reality of actually working there. If your organization does have a beautiful physical space but with an unpleasant culture and a set of tools that look like the equivalent of Tetris for Nintendo (great game but come on . . .), then you are working for a physically emerging organization. Examples of organizations in this category include DuPont, Hershey, and Macy's.

Technologically emerging organizations tend to offer the latest and greatest tools for employees, which can range from software to hardware. Everything is modern and beautifully designed. These organizations really pride themselves on how tech savvy they are. For example, you might find drones flying around the office, augmented and virtual reality setups, high-tech conference rooms and touchable wall displays, the latest and greatest employee communication tools and videoconferencing solutions, the ability for employees to work with any laptop or mobile device they please, and even a smart office environment that can adapt to how employees work with mood lighting, auto climate controls, and voice commands. Again, all of these things are wonderful to have if the organization invests in the other two environments. Sadly, although these organizations might make you feel like you're in a real-life video game, the employees who work there all sit in their cubicle farms while secretly hoping that they will get jury duty so that they can skip a few days of work. Employees here have very little emotional connection to the people or the organization they work with, and they are very much uninspired by their physical surroundings. Tools can take an employee experience only so far! Examples of organizations in this category include Visa, Kroger, and Freddie Mac.

Culturally emerging organizations tend to have a great vibe. Employees really like the people they work with, they feel supported, they have a sense of purpose, and managers are genuinely interested in helping them succeed. This is all tough stuff to accomplish! Remember that the cultural environment contributes 40 percent of the overall employee experience. Culturally emerging organizations are the equivalent of being in a relationship with someone whom you really like and perhaps even love but are not willing to marry. Employees at culturally emerging organizations tend to stay longer than employees at technologically or physically emerging organizations. But still, eventually employees become quite frustrated with actually doing their jobs, and the physical space makes them feel uninspired. The great news for culturally emerging organizations is that if they have indeed figured out the most difficult piece of the puzzle, investing in the physical and the technological environments will seem like a cakewalk in comparison! Examples of organizations in this category include MassMutual, United Airlines, and Four Seasons Hotels.

Next we have organizations that focus on two out of the three environments, which, depending on those combinations, I classify as engaged, empowered, or enabled organizations. Today this can be seen as quite an accomplishment and a long ways away from being either in Experienced or Emerging. You may notice that the words used to describe these organizations are all positive (as are the ones earlier) despite the fact that organizations might be lacking in various areas. Originally I considered using negative terms to focus on what organizations were lacking. But that's neither inspiring nor effective, which is why I took the more optimistic route, because even though many organizations out there aren't perfect, they are indeed trying and moving in the right direction.

Let's look at these three types of organizations in more detail.

Engaged

These types of organizations do a good job of focusing on the cultural and physical environments that create employee experiences. This means that they execute on all or most of the CELEBRATED culture (see Chapter 7) and the COOL physical space (see Chapter 5) attributes. Again, the cultural environment is the most challenging one to execute on. In engaged organizations you will find employees who have a sense of purpose, managers who act as coaches and mentors, a flatter organizational structure, and physical workspaces that are modern, are beautiful, and focus on creating multiple floor plans. The big challenge for engaged organizations is providing employees access to the right tools to do their jobs effectively. Although engaged organizations have gone quite far with how well they are able to execute on the cultural and the physical space, not having a great technological environment holds both of these other two environments back. For example, organizations that try to abolish annual reviews, offer amazing management training solutions, or enable real-time communication and collaboration will find that these are not possible and are not as effective without being supported by great technologies. If you look at the physical environment, you can't enable flexible work, Activity Based Working, or any type of effective employee mobility without having the right technologies in place. Based on this it's not hard to see how poor technology can negatively affect both the cultural and the physical environments.

Remember, technology is the glue that holds the organization together, and it's what allows many of the themes discussed in this book to actually manifest. Engaged organizations struggle with trying to execute on employee experience simply because they don't have all the tools to do so. Examples of organizations in this category include Mars, General Mills, and Nestlé.

Empowered

If your organization has a great technological and cultural environment but lacks in the physical environment, then it is classified as being empowered. Empowered organizations can actually be extremely effective because employees love the people they work with and the company they work for, and they have access to technology that enables them to do their best work. Still, even in these types of organizations, the employee experience could be improved by investing in the physical environment that employees actually work in. As we saw in the first half of the book, the physical space is a crucial environment to invest in. In empowered organizations you will still find plenty of cubicles and closed offices that dominate the overall office design, which oftentimes can leave employees feeling a bit uninspired, unengaged, and unmotivated. In the case of Sanofi mentioned in Chapter 5, we also saw how having a physical environment layered with cubicles and offices reserved for executives can contribute to a strict hierarchy, thus negatively affecting culture. Remember that the physical environment is the easiest way for us to determine the values and vibe of an organization. The good news is that making changes to the physical workspace is probably the easiest thing (out of the three) to do. Not only that but also it can also be quite fun. Examples of organizations in this category include IBM, Disney, and MasterCard.

Enabled

These types of organizations are great at the physical and technological environments, but sadly, when it comes to culture, they are a bit behind the curve. This means employees have access to the best technologies and work in a beautiful office environment, but the work they are doing feels a bit empty. Many of the human needs of employees are simply not met. The cultural environment is the one that employees care about most, so when it's not being invested in properly, it can really have a negative impact on the employee experience. Enabled organizations are very productive and efficient almost like a modern-day assembly line. Things just get done but at the cost of the overall employee well-being. In these types of organizations employees come to view their jobs as simply a paycheck, one they're happy to receive and work for, but still just a paycheck. As a result burnout happens more frequently, and issues begin to arise with attracting and retaining top talent. Examples of organizations in this category include FedEx, USAA, and Pfizer.

PREEXPERIENTIAL

These are organizations that do quite well on all the employee experience environments but they aren't amazing at them. You can expect to see many of the attributes of COOL spaces (Chapter 5), ACE technology (Chapter 6), and a CELEBRATED culture (Chapter 7) implemented in the organization, which is fantastic. Employees at preExperiential organizations also tend to be quite happy, but when an opportunity comes along to join an Experiential Organization, they will likely make the leap! PreExperiential organizations also start to see a fair amount of the business value associated with investing in employee experience, but as we will see later on, it pales in comparison with what the leading organizations are seeing. If you feel like your organization is doing a good, but not great, job in all three employee experience environments, then you're working for a preExperiential organization. Examples of organizations in this category include Dow Chemical, IKEA, and Whirlpool.

EXPERIENTIAL

This is the cream of the crop. Only 6 percent of the 252 organizations I analyzed fell into the Experiential category. Ultimately these are the

companies that are best at creating an environment where people truly
want, not need, to show up to work. This is the ideal scenario for most
organizations and the employees who work there, which means the organization has a great Reason for Being and has mastered COOL spaces,
ACE technology, and creating a CELEBRATED culture. Experiential
organizations are the ones that have mastered the art and science of
creating employee experiences. As changes in technology, design trends,
and workplace values and attitudes continue to change, the experiential
organizations will undoubtedly have to adapt. I'll look at more of
the business value in Chapter 11. The very best organizations were

	Culture	Technologically	Physical Space
inExperienced	☹	☹	☹
Technology Emergent	☹	👍	☹
Physically Emergent	☹	☹	👍
Culturally Emergent	👍	☹	☹
Enabled	👍	☹	👍
Empowered	👍	👍	☹
Engaged	👍	☹	👍
preExperiential	👍	👍	👍
Experiential	★	★	★

☹ Poor | 👍 Good | ★ Excellent

JACOB MORGAN
© thefutureorganization.com

FIGURE 9.1 The Nine Employee Experience Categories

already listed in Part 2, but examples include Google, Airbnb, Accenture, Linkedin, Microsoft, and Cisco.

Figure 9.1 provides a nice and simple breakdown of all of these.

When looking at these nine categories, it's also important to note that organizations can easily move up and down this list and skip around from one category to another. This isn't simply a linear series of movements. It's quite conceivable that an organization can be classified as Experiential and then, as a result of inaction, slip down to Engaged and then return to Experiential.

CHAPTER 10

Employee Experience Distribution

In Figure 10.1 below you can see the breakdown of how many organizations fall into each type of category but I've also written what percentage of the 252 organizations make up each category below:

1. inExperienced (20 percent)
2. Technologically emergent (3 percent)
3. Physically emergent (6 percent)
4. Culturally emergent (20 percent)
5. Engaged (14 percent)
6. Empowered (4 percent)
7. Enabled (4 percent)
8. preExperiential (23 percent)
9. Experiential (6 percent)

There are a few interesting insights we can draw from this data:

- Almost half (49 percent) of the 252 organizations I analyzed are focusing on either none (20 percent) or one (29 percent) of the three employee experience environments. This is an astonishingly high number.

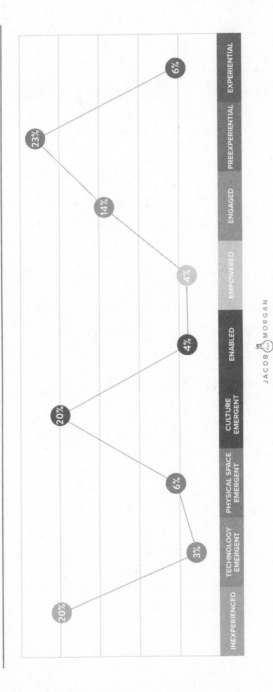

FIGURE 10.1 Percentage of Companies by Employee Experience Category

- Only 22 percent of organizations are focusing on two out of the three employee experience environments.
- Although 29 percent of organizations are indeed investing in all three employee experience environments, only 6 percent of all organizations are considered Experiential, that is, truly delivering great employee experiences.
- Not surprisingly one of the highest peaks on the chart belongs to Culturally Emergent organizations. These are the companies that focus on employee engagement and as you will see in Chapter 11, they see just a tiny fraction of business value as a result. These organizations are investing in short-term adrenaline shot initiatives to boost rankings and scores.

Looking at this data is encouraging but also a bit frightening. It's great that 23 percent of organizations are close to becoming Experiential, but even if they one day did make that leap, the total number of organizations that are truly great at creating employee experiences would still be below 30 percent. That's completely unacceptable and should serve as a wake-up call to employees, managers, and executives around the world that action needs to be taken that focuses on true organizational design. The vast majority of organizations are nowhere near where they should be or where employees will expect and deserve them to be. These are the organizations that will have the hardest time attracting and retaining top talent and delivering on their business objectives.

CHAPTER 11

The Business Value of Employee Experience

Why bother investing in employee experience? Who cares about culture, technology, the physical work environment, and this weird thing called a Reason for Being? Is there really any value to investing in employee experience and becoming an Experiential Organization? As it turns out there is—a lot of it.

Before going on let's do a quick recap of the nine types of organizations so that you can easily reference the list when reading about and seeing the comparisons.

inExperienced—Poor at culture, technology, and physical space

Technology Emergent—Good at technology, poor at culture and physical space

Physically Emergent—Good at physical space, poor at culture and technology

Culturally Emergent—Good at culture, poor at physical space and technology

Enabled—Good at culture and physical space, poor at technology

Empowered—Good at culture and technology, poor at physical space

Engaged—Good at culture and physical space, poor at technology

preExperiential—Good at culture, technology, and physical space

Experiential—Amazing at culture, technology, and physical space

Throughout this section I will also reference nonExperiential Organizations. These comprise all the above categories except the Experiential Organizations (eight categories above). In other words, every organization except for the top 6 percent makes up the nonExperiential group.

To figure out the business impact of employee experience, I looked at four things. The first was anecdotal and observational data that executives shared with me. I had quite a few executives tell me that they observed a more productive workforce, a larger talent pipeline, improved levels of innovation, increased morale, and the like. They didn't have solid data to show this, but they did see and experience it, which was still a positive piece of data to look at. The second thing I did was look at dozens of other lists and rankings of leading organizations to see whether Experiential Organizations appeared on those lists and rankings more often than organizations in other categories. For example, would an Experiential Organization appear on a most innovative company list or a best customer service list more often than any other category of organizations? Next, I looked at metrics around employee turnover, median pay, average profit, employee growth, and average revenue to see how Experiential Organizations compared to others. Last, I wanted to compare stock price performance of various categories of organizations against each other and against the Standard & Poor's 500 and the NASDAQ. Just for fun I also did a comparison of Experiential Organizations and Glassdoor's 2016 Best Places to Work list (for large companies) and *Fortune's* 100 Best Companies to Work For in 2016, which is based on data from Great Place to Work.

Before actually doing any of the data collection for this book, I had a hunch that companies such as LinkedIn, Cisco, Airbnb, and other Experiential Organizations would score high on the Employee Experience Index. I've visited their offices and spoken with their executive teams, so I was aware of the considerable time and investment that these companies were putting into designing employee experiences. I also believed that these companies should appear on various leading organizations lists (and rank higher) more often than other types of companies. However, with research and data analysis, you never really know what the outcome is going to be until you actually see the results. Fortunately in this case, the data showed that the Experiential Organizations absolutely dominate every other category of organizations.

Figure 11.1 below shows the comparison between Experiential Organizations and the other eight types of organizations. You can see how much more often Experiential Organizations appeared on leading lists for innovation, customer service, employee happiness, and employer attractiveness and on a few other miscellaneous lists I found. You can also see how Experiential Organizations compare on various financial and business metrics.

I sliced and diced the data all sorts of ways to compare not only how these nine organizations compare against one another but also how the single top category of Experiential Organizations compares against the other eight categories of organizations combined (simply called nonExperiential). I didn't include every single chart and comparison in this book because that alone would take up many dozens of pages.

For these comparisons you will see various numbers that represent multipliers. This means that if you see a number such as 3.8 it means that the Experiential Organizations appeared on the particular list 3.8× more frequently than the other categories of organizations.

Let's look at these areas in more detail.

CUSTOMER SERVICE

To start I looked at whether Experiential Organizations appeared on various customer service lists more frequently and higher up than other organizations. I looked at a few lists, including the 24/7 Wall Street Customer Service Hall of Fame rankings, Temkin Customer Service Ratings, and the American Customer Satisfaction Index. Experiential Organizations appeared on these lists 2× as often as every other category of organization combined. When comparing Experiential (the best) versus inExperienced (the worst) organizations, this number almost doubled. The lowest gap appeared between the Experiential and the preExperiential (second best) Organizations. In that case the multiplier was 1.3, still a

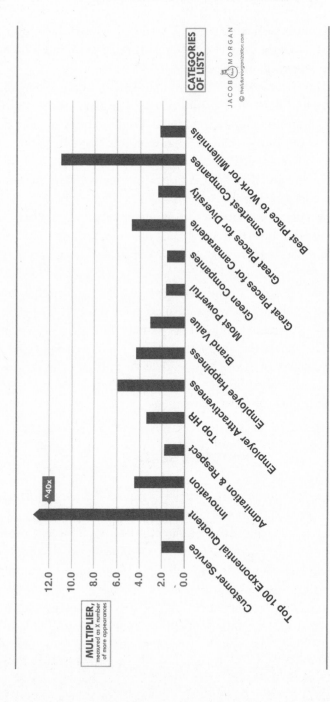

FIGURE 11.1 Frequency of Experiential Organization Appearances on Lists

considerable difference considering we are comparing the very best and the second best categories of organizations. Even a small difference can translate into many millions of dollars for the organization. Customers who receive better service oftentimes spend more and are more loyal to the brand. Not to mention angry customers usually cost the business more because it takes longer to help them—they are also more likely to share their unpleasant experiences with others.

As I mentioned at the start of this book, focusing on employee experience unlocks the discretionary effort of employees, which in turn allows them to provide better customer experiences, so I was glad to see a direct relationship between employee experience and customer service.

INNOVATION

I looked at Fast Company's Most Innovative Companies list, *Forbes's* Most Innovative Companies list, and Boston Consulting Group's Most Innovative Companies list. Experiential Organizations appear on these lists 4.5× more often than nonExperiential organizations (all the other eight categories of organizations combined). Again, when looking at the best versus the worst organizations, this number jumps to almost 7×. This is a whopping number. Clearly the organizations that do an outstanding job of focusing on culture, technology, and the physical environment are also able to innovate at a much higher level. This too makes sense because employees in Experiential Organizations are given the resources needed to bring their best ideas to work every day. Innovation is what leads to new products, services, and partnerships that allow an organization to remain competitive. It's no surprise that innovation is consistently ranked as one of the top priorities for executives around the world. Focusing on employee experience appears to be a great way to achieve this.

EMPLOYER ATTRACTIVENESS

There were many lists here that I had the opportunity to choose from, such as Glassdoor's Best Places to Work, CareerBliss's 50 Happiest Companies, *Fortune's* 100 Best Workplaces for Millennials, LinkedIn's Most

InDemand Employers and Top Attractors, and Brandz Most Valuable Global Brands. Experiential Organizations clobbered every other category of organizations. Experiential Organizations appeared on these lists 6× more often than nonExperiential Organizations, 7.4× more often than inExperienced Organizations, and 2.6× more often than preExperiential Organizations. Employer attractiveness is a critical factor for being able to attract and retain top talent and helps contribute to a larger talent pipeline.

ADMIRATION AND RESPECT

This is very closely related and can in fact overlap with employer attractiveness, but I decided to make it a distinct category. Admired and respected organizations are not only more attractive to prospective and current employees, but they are also looked at as role models for people and other organizations around the world. These are the organizations that we all look up to and try hard to be a part of and have relationships with. Here I looked at lists such as *Forbes*'s Best Employers, *Fortune*'s Most Admired Companies, and *Barron*'s Most Respected Companies. Experiential Organizations appeared on these lists almost 2× more often than nonExperiential Organizations. Looking at the data, it appears that organizations that invest in great experiences for their employees are also widely admired and respected. I don't believe this is a coincidence.

BRAND VALUE

How valuable is your brand? *Forbes* and BrandZ both have lists that measure and look at the overall value of a brand. Experiential Organizations appeared on these lists over 3× more often than nonExperiential organizations. Once again when looking at the best (Experiential) and the worst (inExperienced) categories of organizations, the best appeared on these lists a staggering 10× more often. Yet again it appears that organizations that invest in creating great experiences for their employees are able to build more valuable brands. This too makes sense because in these types of organizations employees are willing to do their absolute best to contribute to value. Being a valuable brand isn't just about getting the most customers or selling the most products. It's also about taking care of your people.

OTHER LISTS

These were some of the main categories I looked at, but there were many other lists that I used to see how much more often Experiential Organizations appeared on them when compared with other categories or organizations. Some of these other lists included Best Places to Work For Millennials, CareerBliss's 50 Happiest Companies, Massachusetts Institute of Technology's 50 Smartest Companies, Green Companies, *Fortune*'s 50 Best Workplaces for Camaraderie, *Fortune*'s 50 Best Workplaces for Diversity, and Workforce 100 (top human resources companies). In every one of these lists, the Experiential Organizations appeared on them between 2× and 11× more often than any other type of organization.

I also looked at a new list created by Salim Ismail based on his book *Exponential Organizations*. These types of organizations are defined as ones "whose impact (or output) is disproportionally large—at least 10× larger—compared to its peers because of the use of new organizational techniques that leverage accelerating technologies." Ismail and his team devised a framework based on 10 attributes, and then they evaluated organizations around the world and created a ranking.[1] Naturally I was curious to see whether Experiential Organizations are also more likely to be Exponential Organizations. It turns out they are. In fact, Experiential Organizations appeared on Salim's list almost 40× more often than any other category of organization that I developed. This is a staggeringly high number, which leads me to believe that the only explanation here is that organizations that invest in employee experience are clearly making a dramatic business impact. It's also important to point out that Ismail's list of the top 100 Exponential Organizations also included much smaller companies, such as Indiegogo, which has around 100 employees; Tumblr with around 400 employees; and Reddit with under 100 employees. There are also plenty of organizations on that list that most people in the world have never heard of, such as Studio Roosegaarde, Enevo, and Yik Yak. I mention this because smaller organizations and start-ups are notoriously known for being more disruptive, agile, innovative, and forward thinking. Still, despite being compared to some of these smaller organizations around the world, the Experiential Organizations dominated the competition.

But just to be safe let's also look at the financial and business side of things.

NOTE

1. Ismail, Salim. *Exponential Organizations: Why New Organizations Are Ten Times Better, Faster, and Cheaper than Yours (and What to Do about It)*. New York: Diversion Books, 2014.

CHAPTER 12

Business Metrics and Financial Performance

Comparing the nine categories on these lists clearly reveals some interesting insights. However, I wanted to take this one step further and look at some financial data and business performance metrics. I looked at data provided by organizations such as Yahoo! Finance, PayScale, and *Fortune*. Although I couldn't find every metric for every company, I was certainly able to cover the vast majority of them. I compared Experiential Organizations with other categories based on employee turnover, median pay, revenue per employee, and profit per employee. Figure 12.1 looks at Experiential Organizations versus nonExperiential, and Figure 12.2 provides a breakdown of how Experiential Organizations perform versus all the other categories of organizations.

Experiential Organizations had 20 percent fewer employees, 40 percent lower turnover, 1.5× the employee growth, 2.1× the average revenue, 4.4× the average profit, 2.9× more revenue per employee, and 4.3× more profit per employees when compared with nonExperiential Organizations. I'd recommend you reread that last sentence a few times and let those numbers sink in. Looking at these numbers also makes it quite clear that Experiential Organizations are also the most productive. This should convince even the most skeptical reader or executive that investing in employee experience does have a significant financial impact on the organization. Another interesting thing to note is that, perhaps

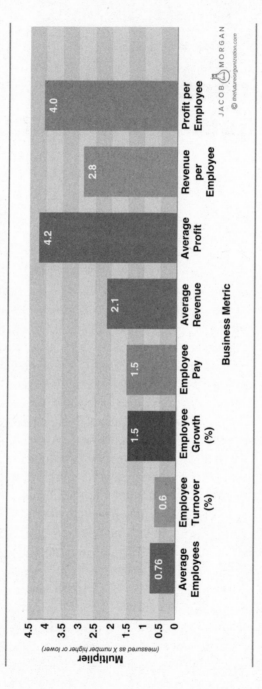

FIGURE 12.1 Business Metrics for Experiential Organizations

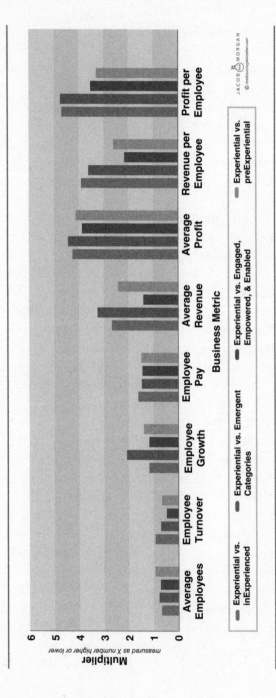

FIGURE 12.2 Business Metric Comparison by Organizational Category

not coincidentally, Experiential Organizations also pay their employees 1.6× more than the nonExperiential Organizations.

Let's say we had two organizations, ACME A (representing Experiential Organizations) and ACME B (representing nonExperiential Organizations). Applying the numbers from the opening of this chapter, Table 12.1 shows how that would translate for two fictitious organizations.

Of course these are completely made-up numbers, but it's easy to see how the impact here can be in the billions of dollars.

To drive this point across even further, I also compared stock price performance of the various categories of organizations and included the Standard & Poor's (S&P) 500, NASDAQ, Glassdoor's Best Places to Work 2016 list (for large companies), and *Fortune's* 100 Best Companies to Work For in 2016 (from Great Place to Work). To do this I looked at the stock price of all the included organizations, from January 2012 through October 2016, and assumed a starting investment of $1,000 for all the categories of organizations. I looked at this in two ways. In Figure 12.3 you can see that I grouped some categories together based on how many of the employee experience environments they were investing in (culture, technology, and physical space). This means that all the Emergent organizations were grouped together, and the Engaged, Empowered, and Enabled organizations were grouped together. In Figure 12.4 everything is broken down individually.

Some of the Experiential Organizations were also part of Glassdoor's and *Fortune's* lists, but regardless, the Experiential Organizations outperformed everyone by a considerable margin. Looking purely at stock price performance, the results aren't exactly what you would expect. Although Experiential Organizations outperformed everyone else, there were some surprises. For example, Technologically Emergent Organizations performed better than most other organizations as did the Enabled Organizations (scoring higher than the preExperiential group). Still, we can't simply rely on stock performance alone to justify the investment in employee experience, which is why I also looked at all the other elements above. But, it's reassuring to see that Experiential Organizations outperformed everyone else, even when it comes to financial investment. Although other organizations do see business

TABLE 12.1 ACME A and ACME B Business Metrics

Company	Employees	Revenue	Turnover	Revenue per Employee	Profit	Profit per Employee	Pay per Employee
ACME A	70,000	$10.5 billion	4,000	$150,000	$4 million	$88,000	$95,000
ACME B	100,000	$5 billion	6,700	$50,000	$900,000	$20,000	$63,000

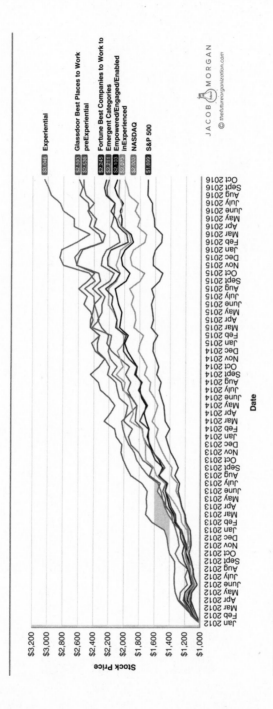

FIGURE 12.3 Category Stock Price Performance with $1,000 Investment

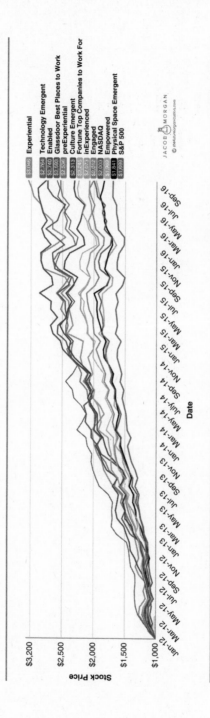

FIGURE 12.4 All Company Stock Price Comparison with $1,000 Investment

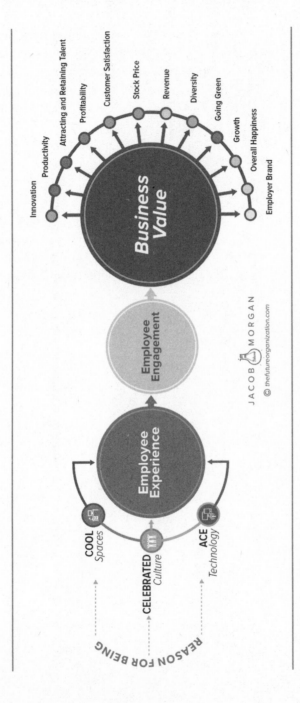

FIGURE 12.5   Employee Experience Business Outcomes

value from investing in even some areas of employee experience, it's quite apparent that there's a bit of a winner-take-all outcome here. The organizations that truly see considerable business value and impact are the ones that excel at all three employee experience environments. They are amazing when it comes to culture, technology, and physical space, and as a result they become amazing companies.

Looking at all of this, it's apparent that Experiential Organizations have higher customer satisfaction scores and rankings; have top-notch innovation practices; are the most attractive and respected places to work; are the most valuable brands; are also smarter, greener, happier, and more diverse; have the best people teams; and have the best camaraderie when compared with any other category of organizations. They are also more likely to deliver higher returns on performance benchmarks when compared with their competition, and they provide a higher return on investment when looking at stock price performance. Surely, this should be enough to convince even the most skeptical of readers, business leaders, and executives that investing in employee experience should be a top priority.

Figure 12.5 will help you conceptualize the employee experience business outcomes that the Experiential Organizations realize. It also puts into context how the concepts in this book fit together. Starting at the very left we have the Reason for Being, which guides how the organization invests in COOL spaces (Chapter 5), ACE technology (Chapter 6), and a CELEBRATED culture (Chapter 7). These are the elements that shape the employee experience, which in turn drives employee engagement. As a result of having a highly engaged workforce, the organization sees tremendous business value. Still, it's not just any organization that sees this business value. It's the one that does an amazing job of investing in employee experience.

CHAPTER 13

The Cost of Employee Experience

One of the things that organizations always get concerned about is cost. Specifically, I hear comments like "We don't have the budget that company X has." This usually happens because of an overemphasis on things such as free gourmet food, designer office spaces, and crazy perks like free dry cleaning, massages, and on-site dog walking. It's true; these things do cost money but the majority of things that shape the employee experience are actually free. What's the cost of treating people well, giving them flexibility and autonomy, hiring a diverse group of people, and giving them the opportunity to learn and grow? How we treat our people is free. Let's look at the 17 variables again below and see which ones require the most significant investment.

The majority of the 17 variables that employees care about most at work actually require little financial investment. Still, there are plenty of things that do cost a considerable amount. You can see a cost breakdown in Figure 13.1. A common example is office space and design. It's not exactly free to transition from cubicles and closed spaces to gorgeous floor plans with wooden floors, tons of natural light, cool-looking conference rooms, and standing desks. General Electric (GE) recently went through this change, and I had the opportunity to visit its new offices in Boston while hosting one of our Future of Work Forums. Walking into the building, you'd think you're visiting a start-up in San Francisco. It turns out that all the employees working in this location used to

	Variable	Cost Level	Type of Cost
Technological Environment	Consumer grade technology	Some costs	Some costs associated with shifting to or creating beautiful modern technologies vs. legacy tools
	Technology available to everyone	Minimal to moderate	Potential cost associated with getting technology to more people
	Technology focused on employee needs	Free	Some time cost associated with understanding how employees work and focusing on the right technologies
Physical Environment	Multiple workspace options	Some or high cost	Costs for design and implementation of new workspaces but costs usually offset by saved real estate expenses
	Physical space reflects the values of the organization	Free or some cost	Potential design changes
	Proud to bring in a friend or visitor	Some or high cost	Potential design changes but no or minimal cost to bring in friends or visitors
	Flexible work and autonomy	Free or minimal cost	No cost for freedom and autonomy but some cost associated with required technology
Cultural Environment	Sense of purpose	Free	No cost for helping people understand how their contribution affects the company and the world
	Being treated fairly	Free	No cost associated with treating people fairly
	Feeling valued	Free	No cost for helping people feel valued
	Managers are coaches and mentors	Free or some cost	No cost for having the right managers in place, some potential cost for training
	Being a part of a team	Free	No cost for employees feeling like part of a team
	Opportunity and resources to learn new things and advance	Free or minimal cost	No cost for giving employees opportunities, potential cost for learning and education programs
	Referring others	Free	No cost for referring others
	Diversity and inclusion	Free (assuming you are hiring people anyway)	No cost for hiring a diverse group of people
	Strong brand perception	Free or minimal cost	Some charge a fee to be evaluated and reviewed for a "best of" list. No cost for treating people well and being ethical
	Employee well-being (physical and mental)	Minimal or some cost	Costs associated with things like gym memberships, classes, and trainings

JACOB MORGAN
© thefutureorganization.com

FIGURE 13.1 Cost of Employee Experience Variables

have offices, and now virtually everyone works in a multiworkspace environment (with mainly open spaces) with free snacks, nice adjustable desks, and beautiful decor. GE, like many other organizations, actually saw a real estate cost savings per square foot by shifting from an all office and cubicle layout to something more modern. It turns out you can actually fit far more people in this type of layout. The real estate cost savings were then used to further invest in things such as free snacks and nice decor. The point is that investing in some of these things doesn't necessarily mean that the organization has to spend more money.

If we're specifically looking at perks, then perhaps no organization is as famous as Google for its massive list of cool things that employees get, ranging from car washes and oil changes to organic grocery delivery to haircuts and salons to free food and even a concierge! What few people realize is that these things are not paid for in full by Google for employees. Companies like Google make these services available and are able to get negotiated rates, but oftentimes employees actually pay for them. For example, it doesn't cost Google anything to allow a mobile car wash and oil change company to come on site to help employees, but it does cost employees to use the services. Making perks available versus actually paying for all of these perks in full are two different things. When most of us hear of all the crazy things that Google does, we assume that the company is paying for everything, but that's not the case. Google focuses on convenience and on making life easier for employees, but it doesn't actually pay for everything. Some things it does actually cover, such as free food, subsidized child care, or shuttle services.

These things can be quite costly to Google, but they are worth it to make life easier for its people. Interestingly enough, according to Laszlo Bock, advisor of Google, the perks aren't the reason why people join or stay at the company. Google does these things for three simple reasons: It's mostly easy, it's rewarding, and it feels right. I know; it might not sound realistic or practical to do all the wonderful things that Google does, but according to Bock, "Remember, that most of these programs are free. They simply require someone at your company to go out and find a vendor who wants to sell to your employees, or organize a lunch, or invite a speaker to visit. Everyone wins."[1] But of course, Google didn't become an Experiential Organization simply by having great perks. It also scored off the charts for diversity and inclusion, employees feeling like they are a part of a team, the ability to learn something new or advance, and several other variables.

However, let's not be so naive as to think that investing in employee experience is quite that simple or quite that cheap. All the forward-thinking organizations highlighted in this book will tell you that they have made considerable investments in everything ranging from people analytics and technology solutions to new management and leadership styles to learning and education programs to completely redesigning and rebuilding their people functions. Organizations like T-Mobile, LinkedIn, Cisco, and others have quite literally held hackathons where they try to break their traditional human resources functions and workplace practices while coming up with better solutions.

The reason why employee experience is such a hard concept for many organizations to wrap their minds around is they are simply not designed to focus on delivering them. In other words, although the cost of implementing the 17 variables discussed earlier might not be that great, the cost to design an organization that is able to implement those 17 variables is. If you recall, at the beginning of the book, we looked at how our organizations have been created based on the ideas that employees are cogs, managers are zookeepers, and work is drudgery. Shifting from an organization that is used to thinking this way to one that thinks about creating employee experiences is definitely a grand challenge, which means resources are necessary. The Experiential Organizations in this book have quite literally had to redesign themselves so that they could be in a position to deliver experiences to their people. There's simply no getting around that.

The interesting thing is that these are crucial business investments that are going to have to be made one way or the other, either now or when your organization is stuck trying to play catch-up to the competition. As shown from all the business and financial analysis in the previous chapter, the return on investment from making these investments in employee experience should be an absolute no-brainer.

NOTE

1. Bock, Laszlo. *Work Rules! Insights from Inside Google That Will Transform How You Live and Lead*. New York: Grand Central, 2015.

PART IV
Building the experiential organization

CHAPTER 14

System 1 versus System 2 Experiences

Daniel Kahneman is one of the world's most renowned psychologists, winner of the Nobel Memorial Prize in Economic Sciences, and author of the best-selling book *Thinking, Fast and Slow*. In his book he describes two types of modes of thought, System 1 and System 2. System 1 thinking is very fast, is instinctive, and doesn't require much focus or attention. It's essentially your brain on autopilot. For example, if I were to ask you, "1 + 1 = ?" you would immediately know the answer. System 2 thinking, on the other hand, is more purposeful, slower, and more deliberate. It's something that requires us to take a step back to process.

As an example consider the following riddle. A bat and a ball costs $1.10. The bat costs $1 more than the ball. How much does the ball cost? The immediate response that most people jump to is 10 cents because $1 plus $0.10 is equal to $1.10, right? But if you take a step back, you will realize that if the ball costs $0.10 and the bat costs $1 more than the ball, then the bat must cost $1.10. However, if you add those two numbers together ($1.10 for the bat and $0.10), then you get $1.20, which is not the correct answer. Only after adding a little bit of brainpower and conscious thought will you be able to figure out that the correct answer is the ball must cost $0.05. This means the bat costs $1.05, and when you add these two numbers together, you get $1.10.

Although Dr. Kahneman explored decision-making and cognitive biases in his book, I think it's great for us to apply this to how organizations approach and design employee experiences. Today, most organizations in the world are stuck with System 1 experiences. That is, they think of employee experience as a checklist of short-term initiatives that they can invest in. Looking at the 17 variables above, many might be tempted to turn this into a checklist that requires little thinking or effort. Just print it out and go down the list. Create a diversity program, implement new training and advancement solutions, give people great tools and a fancy workplace, and boom! You're done. Unfortunately this is exactly the pitfall that many organizations fell into concerning employee engagement. Checklists and steps are great for putting together furniture and baking cakes, but in this case simply ticking off the boxes won't result in great employee experiences.

Every organization has some kind of management training program, but how many organizations offer emotional intelligence and self-awareness modules as a part of that training the way Pandora does?

Every company has a diversity initiative, but how many companies make diversity a part of the executive compensation structure the way Sodexo does?

Every company says it wants to create a sense of purpose, but how many companies actually help every employee truly understand what his or her impact is the way the San Diego Zoo does?

Every company says it wants to give employees great tools to work with, but how many companies truly take the time to understand how employees work, conduct A/B tests, and hold focus groups and interviews the way Facebook does?

Hopefully you get the point that I'm trying to drive home here. The three employee experience environments and the variables that comprise them are of course crucial. These are what employees care about most but they are just ingredients. You've no doubt heard the saying "It's not what you say; it's how you say it," which is applicable here. It's not just about what you do; it's also how you do it. Everyone can implement the concepts in this book, but few can do an amazing job. The key point that I mentioned at the start of this book and one of the big differences of the

Experiential Organizations is that they simply know their people better than any other organization and they genuinely care about them. This is what allows these organizations to move beyond checklists to execute on these variables so well.

Organizations must shift to System 2 experiences, which are conscientious and purposeful efforts that are based on data, design, and employee contributions. I had the opportunity to speak with Marc Merrill, who is the co-CEO and cofounder of the wildly popular Riot Games, which is famous for creating *League of Legends*, one of the most widely played multiplayer games that has ever been created. In 2010 this was a 60-person company, but now it has over 2,000 employees around the world. Riot Games is one of the Experiential Organizations, and it has won numerous other awards for its culture and workplace. When I spoke with Marc about how Riot Games approaches employee experience and why it is able to build such a people-centric organization, his response was quite simple: "If organizations really want to focus on people and make it a priority, then make it a real priority." This type of mentality is what sets the Experiential Organizations apart from all the others. It's the difference between saying something is a priority and actually making it a priority. When an organization truly makes some-thing a priority, you can physically see and feel the changes that take place. It's analogous to saying you want to get in shape versus actually eating right and going to the gym. With that frame of reference, Riot Games is definitely one of the most in-shape companies on the planet!

Out of the 252 organizations I analyzed in this book, virtually all of them are in some way executing on the 17 variables mentioned above. You'd be hard-pressed to find a company today that isn't thinking about new workplace design approaches, challenging conventional management theories, implementing diversity programs, or wanting to treat all employees fairly. It's not like all organizations are villainous, and these three environments and 17 variables are some kind of superhero secrets. They aren't. What sets the Experiential Organizations apart from everyone else isn't so much about what they do as it is about how they do it.

CHAPTER 15

The Employee Experience Design Loop

We have the Reason for Being, the three environments, and the 17 variables that create employee experiences. But, it's still a bit hard to grasp what all of that actually means and how it comes together. The world changes quickly and this means that our organizations have to change quickly as well. Employee experience is a moving target, which means that all the things in this book aren't simply a checklist that you can go through. The way the things in this book get delivered will change dramatically over time. As a result I find it helpful to think of employee experience as an ongoing and never ending back-and-forth interaction between employees and the organization. In other words it's like a dance where both partners need to take the appropriate steps for it to make sense. Except in this dance, the music never stops, and neither does the dancing! This is actually one of the most effective ways for organizations to truly get to know their workforce. Let's start with conceptualizing what this dance actually looks like (see Figure 15.1).

This infinity loop shows an ongoing relationship or a continuum between employees and the organization. There is no break and it's designed to flow a bit like water smoothly around the loop. It's also worth noting that your organization will have many of these design loops going on concurrently, which I'll look at more closely below. While some organizations have purposefully deployed a similar model, others

FIGURE 15.1   Employee Experience Design Loop

have a similar process without actually realizing it. In other words they just haven't taken a step back to visualize and think about what their employee experience design process actually looks like. However, this model resonates with every executive I have shown it to. The full loop has just six sections, which I will describe. You can start anywhere but to make things easier I'll start with the top left.

RESPOND

During this step of the experience loop, employees provide feedback to the organization. In most companies today employees are already talking about what it's like to work there but oftentimes nobody is listening. Employees provide feedback and ideas about anything and everything that can range from a workplace flexibility program to menu items in the cafeteria to management training and development to office design. This can also be extended to performance management as well (and should be). It's a bit analogous to social media. Many brands today are actively engaged with their customers on social channels such as Facebook and Twitter, and they have to respond to all sorts of comments ranging from product issues and outages to compliments to downright angry feedback. These social tools that most of us use in our personal lives act as the delivery mechanism and communication medium between consumers and the organization (in addition to more traditional channels such as e-mail and phone support). The point is that as a customer, you have a direct path to brands, and if you use social technologies, you usually get a faster response.

We need to think of employee feedback in much the same way. Employees can (and should be able to) provide feedback via apps, internal social networks, surveys, focus groups, one-on-one interviews, or any other mechanism that your organization allows and provides for. I will say that it is absolutely crucial to have a real-time feedback mechanism in place.

The important thing here is that this has to happen on an ongoing basis. Simply doing an annual survey to collect feedback is too much of a drawn-out process. With the pace of change that we are all living and working through, the communication, collaboration, and feedback need to happen in real time. Instead of just a single large survey, it makes more sense to leverage multiple feedback points concurrently and continuously. This may include a weekly manager check-in, a monthly pulse survey, a quarterly open discussion, a semiannual experience snapshot, an annual state of employee experience report, and an open platform that employees can use anytime they want. Of course, this is just an example, but it shows that organizations cannot simply rely on one form of response from employees. There should be multiple and they should be used as often as possible. Typically organizations have to actually ask employees for feedback, but why not make it so that employees can share information anytime they want?

Enablers

- Technologies must be in place to allow real-time communication and dialogue.
- Managers must be comfortable receiving and asking for feedback
- Transparency must be the default culture mode.
- The organization must be prepared to take action.

ANALYZE

Next comes the analysis part, where the organization tries to extract as much insight as possible from the feedback to make the next design decision. This part can be rather messy and tricky, and it's where the concept of people analytics comes into play. There is no employee experience without people analytics. This can come in the form of structured data (employee satisfaction, performance, etc.) or unstructured data (observing employees or conducting interviews). The challenge for organizations here is how to make sense of the data that is being collected and then draw some insight from it. This needs to happen as quickly as possible to be able to take action in a timely way. You don't want employees to provide feedback only for it to take the organization six months to analyze and sort through it. Ultimately the big question that organizations need to answer during this stage of the experience loop is "What have we learned from the employee feedback we received?"

Here are some examples of some of the analysis and insight you might glean.

Scenario 1 Analysis Reveals

The highest-performing teams at our company have managers who are more hands-on with career development. Employees appreciate the concern and the effort managers put in and feel like they are genuinely interested and invested in the success of employees.

Scenario 1 Insight for Your Organization

Explore creating a specific training program for your leaders that encourages them to have more discussions around career development with their employees, which includes follow-up discussions. Test how often the discussions should be had, what kinds of conversations should take place, and what types of career advancement employees are looking for.

Scenario 2 Analysis Reveals

Employees don't use the assigned seating areas they have been given. Instead they roam around the office and work in various locations. Employees want more freedom when it comes to their physical space and need a change of scenery during the day to stay engaged and productive. They also like running into new people.

Scenario 2 Insight for Your Organization

Look at creating a physical environment where employees don't have assigned desks but where they can make any space their temporary home. Look at why employees keep moving around and design spaces based on that. Test creating communities or neighborhoods where teams might be colocated or intermingled.

Scenario 3 Analysis Reveals

Annual employee reviews are not viewed as effective by either employees or managers. Employees believe the feedback they receive is too general, too late, and not actionable. Managers don't like stack ranking their employees but feel stuck always having to rate someone below average even though he or she really isn't.

Scenario 3 Insight for Your Organization

Develop a new performance management system where feedback happens in real time and where the information being shared between manager and employee is more goal oriented and purposeful. Leverage technology so that this can happen anywhere and anytime.

Analysis Enablers

Hopefully you see what I'm getting at here. Ideally your organization will also have some concrete numbers for these things so that you can measure effectiveness and improvements in the changes you are making. You might find that 80 percent of your employees want you to increase investment in diversity and inclusion programs and that as a result your retention increases by 10 percent. Whenever possible try to have some numbers in place, again fueled with people analytics.

Enablers

- A people analytics team devoted to analyzing data and gathering insight
- Technologies that allow the data to be aggregated and collected in a uniform way
- Nontechnology-centric ways to collect data, such as focus groups or one-on-one discussions

DESIGN

At this stage employees have provided feedback, and the organization has analyzed the feedback to get some insight. The next stage is actually to create something based on that feedback and insight. What is your organization going to do based on what was learned? If you learned the employees are unhappy with the level of communication and collaboration, what's your solution? If employees want more workplace flexibility, how are you going to make that happen? If you find out that annual employee reviews are dreaded and hated, can you get rid of them, and what will you replace them with? This is the point when the organization actually creates solutions. It's not recommended to dwell too long in the design process because it kills the effectiveness of the entire mechanism. Instead it's better to think of this process as a series of sprints and iterations where the organization can quickly create something, get feedback, and then improve. Speed is more valuable than perfection.

Enablers

- Cross functional team in place to design and create solutions
- A process in place that allows for quick development (for example, the Lean Start-up methodology)

LAUNCH

Here the organization actually releases whatever the *it* actually is. As mentioned at the start of this framework, it could be anything that affects the employee experience with culture, technology, or the physical workplace. As far as how organizations officially launch their initiatives, this can be done in all sorts of ways, including pilot programs, mass announcements across the organization, and creative marketing campaigns. How you decide to release something to your employees is completely up to you.

Enablers

- Communication mechanism to reach employees
- Champions and brand ambassadors to spread the word

PARTICIPATE

Naturally after you launch something what comes next is participation. After the organization announces and implements something, such as a new management training program, flexible work initiative, or workplace layout, employees then use it. This becomes their new reality and their new way of working.

Enablers

- Employee access
- Training and education when necessary

This is the most effective and simplest way for organizations to think about and design employee experiences. Notice that employees make up half of the feedback loop, and the organization makes up the other half. This is quite different from most traditional models, which see the organization own 100 percent of the employee experience while employees have no voice. Thankfully we will never go back to that type of model again. Many organizations use this type of approach without even realizing. However, once you conceptualize this process, it makes it much easier to structure how experiences are designed.

The faster and more frequently you repeat this process, the better. Ideally you will have many of these types of experience design loops happening regularly. You may be looking at a new manager training program while redesigning your physical environment, investing in a diversity initiative, and rolling out a new technology platform. This employee experience design loop is simply a new of way of introducing things into the organization and can be applied to pretty much anything. Let's walk through two real-life examples of this whole process.

EXAMPLE: GENERAL ELECTRIC

This process drove an entire organizational overhaul. General Electric (GE) is a multinational conglomerate with over 300,000 employees around the world. To learn more about the transformation, I spoke with Susan Peters, the chief human resources officer at GE, and Paul Davies, the employee experience leader at GE.

Respond

Employees at GE participate in regular employee surveys and discussions with their managers. Initially, the survey was done every 18 to 24 months, and the discussions with managers weren't happening as often as they should. Naturally this made it challenging to get a pulse on the company. As the company grew it became more difficult to get things done. Too many checks and balances and too much bureaucracy crept into the company. In fact during an interview for *Fortune* magazine, its CEO, Jeff Immelt, said that one of his biggest regrets is that "We just got too slow."[1] One of the things it wanted to do to enhance its overall employee experience was make things simpler, and simplification became one of Immelt's key talking points in his internal and even his external meetings and discussions. Employees were constantly providing feedback to managers and executives that things were too slow, especially when it came to anything related to performance, talent management, and feedback.

Analyze

Through GE's employee survey, it was obvious that employees around the world felt there were many opportunities to reduce the bureaucracy and speed things up. In the past, its employee survey was administered every 18 to 24 months, and it often took months to compile results and communicate them back to employees. By then it was too late to do anything meaningful because the information and the guidance given to employees were already stale. Today, GE still surveys its employees at scale, but results are visible real time. Insights are solicited much more frequently. Leaders can make changes based on the feedback sooner than they have even been able to previously. This went from months, to days. From the feedback that GE received, it became very apparent that it needed to make changes in process, culture, and technology.

Design

The team at GE worked to create something called FastWorks. In its first iteration, it was created as a way of thinking about launching products. As FastWorks evolved, this methodology led to numerous types of projects, not just involving products, but also involving processes. Whether it was FastWorks for projects or the FastWorks Everyday process, the focus was on customer outcomes, testing, and iterating. This evolution of FastWorks helped GE create Performance Development, which is an entire new model of assessing employees. It moved from the Employee Management System (EMS) deployed in 1976 to the new Performance Development. This included new language around feedback, a new time orientation (real-time vs. once a year), a new tone, getting rid of ratings, and deploying a new tool called PD@GE that enabled real-time feedback between employees and managers.

The FastWorks methodology looks like this:

1. Problem statement
   - Identify and try to articulate customer challenges or opportunities.
2. Leap-of-faith assumptions
   - Validate leaps of faith—get customer input early.

3. Minimum viable products (MVPs)
   • The fastest way to get feedback
4. Learning metrics
   • Get feedback from customers to understand whether you are making progress toward their goals.
5. Pivot or persevere
   • Based on customer feedback and learnings, continue to your goal or iterate on your process.

Through this process GE tested a series of assumptions throughout 2014 in what it called a component MVP. In the fourth quarter of 2014, it launched a much larger, integrated MVP, designed based on those learnings of the Performance Development approach. Businesses volunteered to be part of this MVP test. GE identified and tested assumptions in smaller- and bigger-scale experiments with close to 6,000 employees in this MVP. This is a small group compared with the 170,000+ employees globally who used the EMS. But, FastWorks taught them that if something doesn't work for 6,000 people, it definitely won't work for 170,000 people.

To summarize, FastWorks is the overall methodology to simply launch new products and experiment and test to create the most value for customers. Performance Development came about through a FastWorks approach. It is an overhaul of assessing and developing employees, and PD@GE is an app that employees use to provide feedback to one another, track ongoing priorities, and capture important conversations, or touchpoints.

Launch

GE introduced PD@GE and FastWorks in a phased approach, which looked like this:

End of 2012–2013: Test and introduce FastWorks for major projects
2013–2014: Scale FastWorks across businesses and project teams
2014: Introduction of growth boards, a governing mechanism with a rigorous, question-based approach to capital and resource allocation

and customer validation, and introduction of the GE Beliefs, to define the way the company thinks and acts. GE also launched a pilot of Performance Development to 30,000 employees and continued to learn and scale until the global announcement in 2016.

2015–2016: Scaling of FastWorks across all GE employees, as part of a larger culture change, by translating FastWorks principles for everyday use to simplify the way employees work, and focusing on testing and learning early and often with customers, to become a faster, agile, simpler, and more customer-driven organization.

PD@GE was introduced to various business populations as it was scaled across the company. There were marketing materials, including digital signage, posters, and the like. In 2016, when Performance Development was announced as the single approach to employee development, Susan Peters, the chief human resources officer, made the announcement through push notification using the PD@GE app.

FastWorks has been guiding GE's approach to Performance Development since its inception when the HR team started with mapping out the problem through the eyes of customer segments (managers, employees, and the senior leaders who represent the organization) and defining the vision statement. (approximately 2014). Success was measured in terms of the impact on customers (managers, employees, and the organization).

Participate

Employees participate in PD@GE (the app and desktop tool) by capturing touchpoint conversations with managers, sending insights to colleagues, and continuously tracking or modifying their priorities. Here are two scenarios for employee use of the PD@GE app.

Option 1 (an employee experiencing a Performance Development priority-setting touchpoint): An employee at GE wants to walk through the projects they are working on to discuss priorities with their respective manager. As they do this the manager asks some challenging questions, such as "What's the solution you're providing for your customer?" "Who's the end user of this?" "Is it adding value to them?" "How do you know?"

These are all focused on value and impact versus tactical to dos and tasks. As the employee leaves the meeting with the manager, they have a 10-minute window before another upcoming meeting, so they open their PD@GE app and add new priorities based on the conversation. A key thing to point out is that employees are trusted by their managers to update their priorities. They also send their manager an insight that was learned from the conversation.

Option 2 ("imagine" scenario): Similar to option 1, imagine walking into your manager's office. You have a list of the goals that you want to set for yourself. You have the tactical elements set up, and you are ready to start working on them. You think you'll just need to report them out to your manager and then be on your way. Instead, your manager reviews the goals and then asks the same strategic questions as in option 1. You realize that you are missing feedback on one of your priorities. However, your manager thinks it has potential but pushes you to test it with your customers and then come back with any adjustments based on their needs.

As you leave the meeting, you walk down the hall to your next meeting. After your meeting ends, you feel a buzz in your pocket coming from your phone. You receive a push notification saying, "You have just received an Insight." You open the app and see that your manager sent you a Continue Insight that says: "Thanks for bringing your goals to our meeting. They were well thought out and aligned to our overall strategy. I look forward to hearing the results of the tests that you'll run with your customers based on that one priority that didn't have direct input just yet. Let's set up another meeting when you feel you have enough detail to adjust or change that priority." You've just lived and breathed Performance Development at GE. You collaborated with your manager to create value for your customer. You've received real-time feedback that has helped you learn and grow. And you're empowered to try something new, test it, learn from it, and adjust it.

The scope of this project was grandiose to say the least, but it shows how a large organization like GE was able to leverage the employee experience feedback loop to drive change and test ideas based on employee feedback and insight.

EXAMPLE: AIRBNB

Airbnb is a marketplace that allows people to rent out local listings in almost every country around the world. Today the company has over 2,000 employees around the world and is a great example of how the employee experience design loop can be applied to something rather unconventional...food. David McIntyre, Airbnb's global director of food (how awesome is that?), explained how the company's approach works in the context of the employee experience design loop. It's important to point out that at Airbnb, food isn't a perk or an amenity. It's a purposefully designed strategic investment for the company. Its approach to food can be summed up in one word, *Sobremesa*, which is a Spanish word meaning "the time you spend at the table after you finish eating." At Airbnb food is a way to get employees to talk, engage, share, collaborate, and build community.

Respond

Airbnb provides three meals a day for all of its employees. A menu is sent out via e-mail before each meal, and at the bottom of these e-mails, employees can click on a feedback link. There's also a dedicated e-mail address for the food services team that employees can use anytime they want. Finally, the Airbnb team also conducts a food and beverage satisfaction survey around once a year. Using these mechanisms (in addition to some in-person conversations), employees provide all sorts of feedback to the team, which ranges from general praise to specific requests for things such as more gluten-free options.

Analyze

The food services team considers all the various feedback mechanisms and then looks at the collected data to determine a few things. First is general satisfaction of the food and beverage offerings to determine whether employees are happy with what they receive. Second is the balance of food options. In the surveys Airbnb seeks to balance healthful, indulgent, familiar, and exotic options. Ideally, it would see its menu show around 25 percent in each of the four categories. Third is the usage patterns of the employees: which meals and how many meals they consume in the office. Fourth, David and his team look at how food affects the culture of the company by asking employees where they connect with their peers most often. Last, Airbnb tries to determine how food affects the overall outcomes of the business by looking at things such as productivity, recruitment, and retention. According to its data over 90 percent of employees say that the food and beverage programs help make them more productive, and over half acknowledge that food affects their decision to work at and stay at Airbnb. Although Airbnb does look at quantifiable data, sometimes it also makes decisions based on observations. For example, it might notice that it is getting a lot of e-mails requesting more vegetarian options, so then that becomes a priority item.

Design

David and his team have a very solid understanding of what the employees at Airbnb want and need when it comes to food and beverages. As much of their food as possible comes directly from farmers, so they know what is in season and what is coming in. The menus are designed quarterly based on the four seasons of the year, and everyone from the chef to the dishwashers provides feedback on the menu choices. The team considers everything from halal and vegetarian options to special gluten-free or even paleo diets, not to mention food allergies that some employees might have. The team, of course, must also look at costs and what is practical and feasible.

The results from the food and beverage satisfaction surveys are always shared with all the employees so that they have transparency about why certain decision were made and why some options were chosen. Each Airbnb office has its own chef (whenever possible), which means that each is responsible for his or her own cuisine based on local preferences. There isn't a single head chef for the entire company. This allows for much greater personalization.

Launch

Launching the new food items is a matter of the chefs preparing, cooking, and placing the food out for employees to eat. It's amazing how much work goes into this. I've visited its headquarters in San Francisco a half dozen times and am always blown away by the quality and diversity of options. It also has a pastry chef who devilishly creates little treats that get wheeled around on carts throughout the day. The main mechanism for how it actually launches food is its opt-in e-mails, which showcase the menus of the day along with all the ingredients that are used in preparation. A picture of a relevant Airbnb listing also accompanies each menu to help remind employees of the mission of "Belong Anywhere." This means that if the menu is inspired by Filipino food, employees will see a listing from the Philippines.

Airbnb also offers cooking classes and little pop-up shops in various parts of its offices. For example, it's common to get an e-mail that says something along the lines of "Today from 2 to 3 PM we are offering matcha tea lattes in the upstairs kitchen. Come grab one and say hello to your coworkers!"

Unlike traditional products or services that take time to create and are launched once, food is something that all employees consume globally and multiple times a day.

Participate

This is the fun part! Employees get to eat all the amazing things that David and his team work so hard to create and to prepare. Then they provide feedback to the team and the cycle repeats!

The employee experience design loop can be applied to any situation where employees and the organization collaborate and communicate to create something, solve a problem, or identify an opportunity. Oftentimes organizations are stuck in the *design for* mind-set, and this approach really forces them to shift their perspective to the *design with* mind-set. It's something many of the Experiential Organizations practice regularly, and it can also be called *cocreation*. This explains why the likes of Google, Airbnb, and Facebook are always ranked as such great places to work (and why they scored so high in the Employee Experience Index). Employees are quite literally involved in designing and shaping their own experiences, and these organizations are obsessed with getting employee feedback. Of course, none of this is possible without an unrivaled level of transparency.

NOTE

1. http://fortune.com/2015/06/03/ge-immelt-chat-transcript/.

CHAPTER 16

The Starbucks Model of Transparency

As you think about employee experiences, you might realize that the larger the organization becomes, the more ideas, feedback, and experiences you have to create. If your organization has 5,000 employees and half of them are contributing ideas or providing feedback regularly, that's still many thousands of ideas a year. What about an organization with 10,000 employees, 100,000 employees, or 300,000 employees? All of a sudden things can get a little bit out of control, and the employee experience design loop model starts to break down. Then what's the solution? How can an organization listen to the ideas of many thousands of people and then implement those ideas regularly? The answer is it can't. At least not yet. In the future as we start to see more AI in the workplace, organizations will be able to deliver an amazing amount of customized experiences. Software will "know" all employees, what they care about, what they value, what they want, and what they need individually. That type of granular view of employees is just not possible or practical today. You've heard of all sorts of smart things, such as the Nest Thermostat that knows when you're home, what temperature you like and when, what time you go to sleep, and what overall temperature conditions you prefer your home to be in. Well what if we took that concept and applied it to how you work? AI that knows how you work better than you do!

For many years Starbucks has been a prime example of customer engagement and innovation through something it launched called "My Starbucks Idea." Search for it online and you'll see what I'm talking about. Through this site Starbucks allows all customers around the world to submit ideas for things they would like the company to do or invest in. Although it seems like Starbucks has since throttled back the focus on My Starbucks Idea, there have been hundreds of thousands of ideas submitted by customers. These idea categories range from store atmosphere to social responsibility to food and drink. The way that Starbucks manages all these ideas is through one magical concept, transparency. On the site, customers vote up which ideas they would like to see implemented, and Starbucks lets the community know which ideas are being evaluated, which ideas are being implemented, which ones have launched, and even which ideas haven't gone over well.

With this level of transparency customers are okay with the fact that not every idea or piece of feedback will be implemented because they know why. I like to call this the "Oh, okay" moment. It's when you get a bit wound up about something, and then once you understand the rationale for why something happened the way it did, you relax and say, "Oh, okay."

Starbucks customers know what the company is doing, thinking about, and implementing. Although organizations always talk about transparency, imagine implementing this type of concept inside of your organization that is focused on employees. What would it be like if your people could provide feedback and ideas around culture, technology, and their physical work environment and see which ones are most popular, which the organization is actually thinking about implementing, and which ones haven't worked and why? I haven't seen any organization take it to this level yet. These types of things might happen more informally through discussions or conversations, but I believe implementing this type of concept (powered by technology, of course) would lead to some interesting results. Transparency is the best way to balance employee freedom with organizational control. It's a seesaw that sees transparency as the balance point in the middle. Not every organization is quite ready for this level of transparency, which is understandable. How much transparency should your organization allow for? As much as possible! The image below shows how transparency acts as the balance between employee freedom and organizational control.

Balancing Freedom and Control

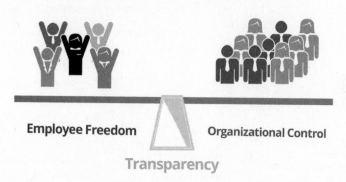

Employee Freedom   Organizational Control

Transparency

© **Jacob Morgan** *(thefutureorganization.com)*

In *Work Rules!* Laszlo Bock, the former senior vice president of people operations at Google, wrote, "If you believe people are good, you must be unafraid to share information with them." At Google as much as possible is "default to open," meaning "make as much information open and accessible as possible." Almost all the entire Google code base, including Search, YouTube, AdWords, and AdSense, is accessible to a newly hired software engineer starting from day one. Its intranet portal, which has all the company road maps and plans along with employee quarterly goals, is also public for any other employee to see. Google also does weekly all-hands meetings for many thousands of employees, and employees have the opportunity to ask literally any question they want to the most senior executives at the company. Nothing is off limits. Google does an excellent job of conveying not only what it is working on but also why it is working on certain things. Bock sums this up brilliantly:

> Fundamentally, if you're an organization that says, "Our people are our greatest asset" (as most do), and you mean it, you must default to open. Otherwise, you're lying to your people and to yourself. You're saying people matter but treating them like

they don't. Openness demonstrates to your employees that you believe they are trustworthy and have good judgement. And giving them more context about what is happening (and how and why) will enable them to do their jobs more effectively and contribute in ways a top-down manager couldn't anticipate.[1]

NOTE

1. Bock, Laszlo. *Work Rules! Insights from Inside Google That Will Transform How You Live and Lead*. New York: Grand Central, 2015.

CHAPTER 17

The Employee Life Cycle

To design employee experiences, we first have to think differently about employees and the journey that they will take with your organization.

The typical employee life cycle follows a process that looks something like Figure 17.1.

Nobody thinks about his or her time at an organization in this way. This isn't really the employee life cycle. This is the organization's version of what it wants the employee life cycle to look like. Right now this journey is very one sided and quite frankly, inaccurate, which means whatever experiences your organization is trying to design aren't based on how things actually work. As an organization you can try to create as many neat little buckets and processes as you want, but remember that they simply reflect how you want things to be, not how they actually are. It's like looking at an organizational chart. You may want your company to function in a nice little pyramid, but anyone with a pulse who has worked for an organization knows that these charts never (and I really mean never) reflect how work gets done and how teams are structured.

Some organizations, such as LinkedIn, have been putting a bit of a modern spin on this to see things from the employee perspective. Nina McQueen is the vice president of global benefits, mobility, and employee experience. She along with Pat Wadors (the chief human resources officer) and the rest of their awesome team have a model they use called the 4-box model. They didn't create this concept but they did adapt it. Not the most exciting name in the world, but hey, it works. Essentially it looks

FIGURE 17.1   Typical Employee Life Cycle

at the four stages that employees go through while working at LinkedIn. The four stages are:

Eager Beaver—You just started the job, are super excited, and feel like you can do anything.

Oh Sh*t (or Oh My)!—Usually around six months in (can be sooner), you hit a wall and believe the job is not what you thought it was, or perhaps the job is too big and overwhelming. You think you aren't cut out for this.

Okay, I'm Starting to Get It—You're able to tackle challenges, complete assignments and big projects, and find your voice. Now you feel like you truly belong.

Master—Now you're almost too good. As a result you get a little bit bored and uninspired with the work you are doing. You may even start to look elsewhere at other opportunities outside of the company.

LinkedIn believes and puts a lot of trust in managers to help guide employees through these four areas, especially the *Oh My!* box. Ideally you should be in all four boxes at the same time. If you find yourself stuck in one of the areas, such as *Master*, then it's your job to speak with your manager or volunteer on something that can help take you back to the *Eager Beaver* box (and you are encouraged to do so).

LinkedIn is among the organizations that are thinking about how to redefine the traditional employee life cycle. The traditional model is still there as a way to help organizations think about talent, but it's becoming a more secondary framework. Your approach may not look like the one that LinkedIn has, but I can guarantee you one thing. It also doesn't look like the one depicted above from decades ago.

These life cycles were great when the organization operated like a finely oiled machine, where everyone went through the same process and did the same thing. This isn't how work gets done anymore. Instead, the life cycle is being replaced or augmented by specific moments.

CHAPTER 18

Moments That Matter or Moments of Impact

Instead of thinking of a traditional employee life cycle, it's more valuable and effective to think of moments that matter or moments of impact. The blurring of our personal and work lives means that these moments also transcend these boundaries. Moments that matter can include things such as your first day at work, having a child, getting promoted, buying a house, leaving the company, or anything in between. By focusing on these moments the organization is able to look at employees as whole individuals with unique experiences as opposed to just employees who are there simply to complete a job. This is what allows organizations to bring a level of personalization to the workplace. Not every organization will have the same moments that matter, but regardless of what they are, every organization can respond by doing something concerning technology, culture, or the physical work environment.

There are three categories of moments that matter, which you can see in Figure 18.1.

SPECIFIC MOMENTS THAT MATTER

These are specific moments in the life of an employee that have clear significance. They include things such as your first day on the job, buying your first house, having a child, and getting promoted. These are

FIGURE 18.1 Types of Moments That Matter

common moments that will most likely be shared across the majority of your workforce. Specific moments that matter are special because they don't happen all the time. They may happen all the time to your collective workforce but not to each employee.

ONGOING MOMENTS THAT MATTER

The continued relationship you have with your peers or managers would be considered an ongoing moment that matters. In other words these moments can't be clearly defined. If one day your manager shows up to work and calls an all-hands meeting just to say thank you for a project you completed, that is not something that is planned yet can have a profound impact on your experience. Similarly, if one day your manager berates you or takes credit for your work, then that too will forever affect your experience at work but negatively. In both of these situations these moments aren't specific things that are planned or designed for. They just happen. These ongoing moments also include how employees interact with technology and the physical workspace that your organization provides.

CREATED MOMENTS THAT MATTER

Company-wide parties, team building events, innovation challenges, or company hackathons are all a part of created moments that matter. These are moments the organization creates because they and the employees feel they are important and are oftentimes focused on a specific business need or challenge.

MOMENTS THAT MATTER AT CISCO

One of the companies pioneering the concept of moments that matter is Cisco. I spoke with its chief people officer, Francine Katsoudas, to learn more about its approach. This all started a few years ago with its Our People Deal, an employee-created concept that outlines what Cisco stands for, what it expects from employees, and what employees can expect from the company. Listening to employees, Cisco realized each employee had different milestones and things he or she cared about that shape his or her experiences. To date, it has 11 moments that matter, each of which has various elements that fall within it. What's fascinating is that these moments came directly from employees who participated in focus groups, discussions, and surveys, during which they candidly shared which moments they cared about most during their career journey. This includes everything from an employee's first interview to his or her last day at Cisco, to celebrating one's birthday with a day off, to having five paid days off (outside of vacation time) to volunteer. In a sense these moments have become the new employee life cycle from the actual perspectives of the people who work there as opposed to how Cisco thinks the employee life cycle should look.

Although Francine and her team helped design these experiences, it is the managers whom Cisco relies on to make the employee experience the best it can be. One particular moment is owned not by a single team or person but by a cross functional team. Each moment has an executive sponsor, a team of experts, and a group of individuals working to design and continuously improve these experiences. Still, it's not as though Cisco doesn't have its own set of challenges. As an organization with over 70,000 employees around the world, making sure that the moments that matter scale across geographies and cultures is not an easy task. Investing heavily in management training and making sure that the relevant teams are global in representation are both crucial things to do.

By focusing on moments that matter, Cisco has created an agile and adaptable model. New moments can always be added or removed based on employee feedback, and each one has a robust road map that connects technology and the human touch. Later in Chapter 25 you will see exactly what these moments at Cisco are.

CHAPTER 19

Moments That Matter and Employee Experience

When you look at the employee experience, which comprises COOL physical spaces (Chapter 5), ACE technology (Chapter 6), and a CELEBRATED culture (Chapter 7), the natural question to ask is how these 17 variables and the Reason for Being fit in with the moments that matter. Are they separate things or do they work together? They are distinct but they work together.

The employee experience environments (and variables) are what I have identified employees care about most. The moments that matter are the specific periods in the life of an employee that are most meaningful and influential. Together, these two things create a powerful combination.

Everything your organization will ever do concerning employee experience will fall into something that is a part of the cultural, technological, or physical environment. Based on the most recent data that I have collected, the 17 variables are the best measurement of what employees care about and value in those three environments. This can and will absolutely change over time. Years ago diversity and inclusion was nowhere near the top of the list, and neither were workplace flexibility, having a manager who acted like a coach and mentor, and a half dozen of the other variables that I explored.

Moments that matter build on this to create something that is specific for your organization and personalized to your employees. Regardless of how your organization approaches this, you will find that not every employee prioritizes the 17 variables that I have identified in the same way. As I mentioned earlier, some examples of key moments might be the first day of work, buying a house, or getting that first promotion. Examples of some of the employee experience variables include feeling a sense of purpose or having a flexible and autonomous work environment. So how do these two things fit together?

The moments that matter are times when you want to incorporate the variables discussed in this book. Let's say you have an employee whose first day is tomorrow. What can do you during that key moment to help convey a sense of purpose and meaning for that employee? Perhaps on day one you can allow that employee to meet one of your customers who has been affected by what your organization does, or maybe that employee meets with a member of the executive team who shares the story and vision of the company and how that employee will play a meaningful role going forward. What about flexibility and autonomy? For an employee to be able to enjoy life and participate in the many meaningful moments he or she will have with family, such as buying that first house, having the first child, taking and picking the child up from school, and attending soccer games, workplace flexibility and autonomy are crucial. I can't tell you how many people I've come across who can't help but neglect their families because of fixed schedules and command-and-control management styles.

Organizations should identify these moments that matter and then infuse them with the 17 employee experience variables that are discussed in this book. This is exactly what some of the top Experiential Organizations, such as Cisco, LinkedIn, Adobe, and Accenture, have been doing. I can't tell you what these moments that matter are going to be inside of your organization, but thankfully we all know who can, your employees.

This doesn't need to be a complicated and convoluted process. It's a bit like going out on a date. When most people first start dating, they're oftentimes stuck worrying about what to say. The common dating advice passed around is simply to ask the other person about himself or herself as a way to start the conversation. Use this same approach to learn about your employees. Start by asking a simple question, something along the lines of "During your time at our organization, what particular moments or events have shaped your experience the most?"

CHAPTER 20

The Employee Experience Pyramid

I like to think of employee experience as a pyramid that has various tiers that sit on top of one another (see Figure 20.1).

At the base of the pyramid, we have the Reason for Being, which provides the foundation for how the organization approaches and thinks about employee experience. The Reason for Being is ultimately what connects the people to the organization. For example, look at the Reason for Being for Starbucks (a preExperiential Organization), which is "To inspire and nurture the human spirit – one person, one cup, and one neighborhood at a time." When an organization makes a statement like that, you can and should expect that it has an attitude of caring about its people. Of course, there are plenty of exceptions to this. Look at Apple, which scored in the Experiential Category yet has absolutely no Reason for Being. Its current mission statement is: "Apple designs Macs, the best personal computers in the world, along with OS X, iLife, iWork and professional software. Apple leads the digital music revolution with its iPods and iTunes online store."

Compare that with the Reason for Being Steve Jobs first instilled at the company in the 1980s, which was "To make a contribution to the world by making tools for the mind that advance humankind."

Those are two radical statements and commitments from the same organization, and it's not surprising that so many people today believe

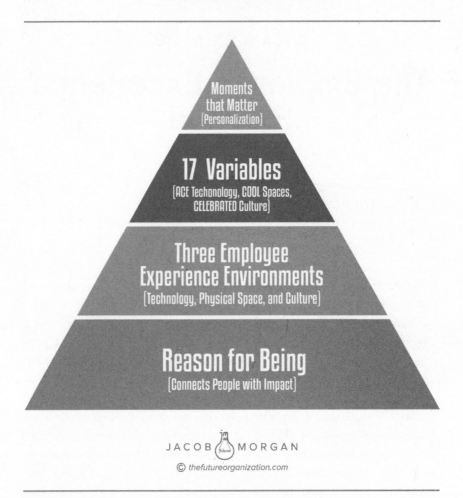

FIGURE 20.1   The Employee Experience Pyramid

that Apple has lost its way and is struggling with creating new and innovative products. A powerful Reason for Being forces the organization to commit to delivering great employee (and almost always customer) experiences. It makes the organization accountable, especially in this transparent world we live in.

On top of that we have the three employee experience environments, which are culture, technology, and the physical environment. Everything and anything your organization will ever do concerning employee experience will fall into these three environments. This includes compensation and benefits enhancements, flexible work programs, management training, the tools that employees use to get their jobs done, and everything in between. Thinking of employee experience as a combination of these three environments will dramatically help simplify things.

Then we have the 17 variables that make up those environments, which are COOL spaces (Chapter 5), ACE technology (Chapter 6), and a CELEBRATED culture (Chapter 7). Based on my analysis these are the 17 things that employees care about and value most in their organizations. Through investments in people analytics, your organization will be able to determine any changes in these 17 variables over time. Remember that as the world continues to evolve, so must our approaches to and strategies for providing employee experiences.

At the very top of the pyramid, we have the moments that matter. These allow organizations to personalize the employee experience as much as possible. Organizations do this by identifying the key moments in the life of an employee and then infusing the 17 variables into those moments whenever possible. Leveraging multiple feedback mechanisms allows organizations to more effectively and accurately identify these moments. The moments will differ by organization, which is why it's so crucial to ask employees, and to keep asking them, because these moments can absolutely change.

The employee experience pyramid helps put into perspective how the various elements fit and work together, kind of like a jigsaw puzzle. The best companies execute on all of these things.

CHAPTER 21

What about the Actual Work?

One thing is quite obviously missing from all the discussions around employee experience: the actual work that employees have to do. Put more directly, the question that people oftentimes ask me is "How does the actual work impact the employee experience?" It's a very fair question to ask, and the work does affect the experience. However, it wasn't included in this book for one crucial reason. In almost all cases the organization doesn't control the work you do, but it controls the environment in which it gets done. Usually, you decide on the work.

When you apply for a job, you should have a pretty good sense of what the role is, what you will be doing, and what's expected of you. In other words, you are picking the job, and there shouldn't be that many surprises. If you get hired in sales, chances are you won't get asked to go fix a server issue, and if you get hired in customer service, you most likely won't have to give a presentation on sales performance. Of course, I'm not naive enough to think that we all have the luxury of leisurely picking our jobs and the organizations we work for. Plenty of people around the world are simply willing to take any job to pay their rent. Even in these situations the environment in which we work has an impact, and even in these situations the employee knows what he or she is getting into. This means that employees need to have a certain level of self-awareness to determine their careers, the organizations they want to work for, and the roles they want to have. Of course when first entering the workforce this is something most of us struggle with but must also develop over time.

If you think about it, the organization can't change the work you do. If you get hired as an engineer, the code needs to be written. If you're hired as a sales professional, the deals need to be closed. If you get hired as a customer service representative, then the customers need to be helped. In this case the variable isn't the actual work itself; it's how the work gets done. I see this all time when speaking with employees at different organizations who have the same roles and functions. The jobs and tasks are virtually identical, but the environment in which they are done is different. This, of course, should come as no surprise. In fact many of us have experienced this in the course of our careers. I certainly have. Perhaps you were on the marketing team of a particular organization, and after a year or so of working there, you started to hate your job. You didn't feel appreciated, your manager didn't care about you, and you didn't feel like you were having much of an impact. As a result you switched jobs and worked for a similar organization where your job was pretty much the same. A year goes by and you're much happier. Your manager is always checking in on you to see how you're doing, frequent socials with your team members are organized to create a stronger employee bond, and you really feel like you're making a difference. The work itself didn't change, but the environment in which the work was done changed. That's what made the impact.

As I was going through the data I collected, I noticed many instances where organizations in the same industries that did pretty much the same thing scored quite differently on the Employee Experience Index. How come? I suppose it is possible that some organizations are just so amazing at always picking the exact right people that they always have a perfect match between what the employee wants, needs, and expects and what the organization actually delivers. I have yet to meet organizations like this, and just like Bigfoot or the Loch Ness Monster, chances are they are fictional creatures. Everything I have researched and seen points to the environments in which the work gets done as the cause for such variations in score.

Let's compare Mercedes-Benz, a company that scored in the lowest category, inExperienced, and Toyota, a company that scored in the

Engaged category. Both companies essentially do the same thing. They manufacture, market, and sell cars. The difference is that Toyota does a much better job of influencing how employees' jobs get done and how they feel about doing those jobs. When comparing the data, Toyota scored just slightly higher than Mercedes in most of the variables, but there are two areas where the score difference was significant. Employees at Toyota feel more valued, and they feel like they are being treated more fairly than the employees at Mercedes. Even though employees at both organizations may have identical jobs, their experiences are quite different.

Another good example is PepsiCo and Coca-Cola. Again, they're two organizations that pretty much do the same thing: manufacture, market, and sell food and beverage products. PepsiCo scored in the lowest category, inExperienced (sorry, Pepsi lovers), and Coca-Cola scored in the Engaged category. Why? Coca-Cola scored much higher in the areas of learning and development opportunities, working in a physical space that reflects the values of the organization, and feeling proud to bring in friends or visitors to the workplace. Yet again we see the job is the constant and the environment is the variable.

This trend has appeared across many of the 252 organizations that I have collected data on. The job and the work are constant, and although they do affect the employee experience, that comes from your choice. This is why it's so crucial for all of us to have a great understanding of who we are, what we are good at, and what we want to do. Aside from switching careers or jobs, the only thing the organization can shape is how the work gets done, not what the work is.

CHAPTER 22

Who Owns the Employee Experience?

It's easy to say that the employee experience is owned by everyone, but from what I have observed, when something is said to be owned by everyone, it's really owned by no one. Instead, I prefer to look at employee experience as something of a ripple effect that starts with the most senior leaders at the organization and extends to every employee regardless of role or seniority. You can see what this looks like in figure 22.1 below.

INITIATED BY THE CEO AND EXECUTIVE TEAM

The entire employee experience of the organization starts with the Reason for Being and the values that the organization chooses to espouse. This starts at the absolute top of the organization with the CEO and every member of the executive team. This can be thought of as the foundation on which the employee experience house is built. The CEO and members of the executive team need to embed this Reason for Being into their talking points both publicly and privately. They also need to make this a part of how they work, communicate, and interact with employees, customers, and the public. Basically, the CEO and the executive team are supposed to be the biggest evangelists of this. When you look at Experiential Organizations, such as Facebook or Google, they all have CEOs who are amazing champions of making sure that their people are

JACOB MORGAN
© thefutureorganization.com

FIGURE 22.1   Employee Experience Ownership Ripple

taken care of and that their organizations are places where employees truly want to show up to work. This can't happen effectively if the top executives aren't on board.

One of my favorite examples here comes from John Legere, the charismatic magenta- and Batman-loving CEO of T-Mobile, a wireless provider with over 54,000 employees. Everything about John is unconventional, including how he encourages drinking games around his competitors' earnings calls, regularly responds directly to customers on social media with his e-mail address, hosts a regular Sunday cooking show on Facebook Live, or has his entire wardrobe T-Mobile branded, down to his magenta Converse shoes. John also has millions of people around the world who follow him on social media and interact with him regularly. Knowing all of this, it should come as no surprise that John has some pretty strong opinions about employee experience (and many other things!).

Ever since he took over as CEO, he's been on a mission to not only connect with and inspire his employees but also improve their experiences by removing as many of their pain points as he possibly can. In a conversation I had with Marty Pisciotti, VP, employee careers, human resources at T-Mobile, he told me that during John's first few weeks at T-Mobile, he was already on the road meeting employees in the regions to hear firsthand about their challenges. At one of the first large sales employee meetings, he held an open mic so that employees could ask him any question they wanted. The first few questions were the predictable safe questions that any employee could ask without getting in trouble. After a few of those, John got up, walked over to the mic, and announced, "I want every question after this to be something that will make you think that the person who asked it will be fired." Employee experience is so crucial to John that all of his executives and managers know the mantra to "listen to your frontline [employees who directly interact with the customers], shut up, and do what they say." It's not often that you hear about a CEO who so openly wants to challenge conventional management and workplace practices.

OWNED BY THE PEOPLE TEAM

At places like General Electric and streaming Internet radio company Pandora, employee experience is a role that exists under the human resources (HR) department, and the people who lead employee experience report to a chief HR officer. I've also seen scenarios where heads of employee experience operate a role that runs in parallel with HR, and the chief employee experience officer is a direct peer. There are all sorts of combinations you can come up with for how the role and the functions are structured. Even all the top companies don't have similar approaches. Airbnb has a chief employee experience officer and someone else responsible for more traditional HR. Adobe has an executive vice president of both customer and employee experience. At Cisco there's a chief people officer, and at Accenture there's a chief leadership and human resources officer. The point is that all of these models and scenarios are perfectly acceptable, and they can all work (and they do). There isn't a one-size-fits-all approach as far as what the makeup of these teams looks like from a function and role perspective.

Ultimately this group of people is responsible for guiding employee experience across the organization. They usually start the discussions, come up with strategies for how to execute on experience, test ideas, provide guidance based on people analytics, and otherwise take ownership of making sure the entire company champions employee experience. These guys are like the secret task force that the company can turn to. This doesn't mean that they have to make all the decisions or that nothing gets done without their input. It simply means that they help guide and steer the ship, but everyone participates in getting it to the right destination. The main goal of the people team is to help put employee experience at the very center of the organization.

DRIVEN BY MANAGERS

Every manager at an organization is responsible for driving and creating employee experiences. This means helping make sure the 17 variables above are being implemented and recognized by employees, identifying the key moments that matter, getting to know the whole employee, and encouraging employees to speak up and help shape their own experiences. When looking at the future of work, the manager isn't the one who sits at the top of the pyramid. The manager is the one at the very bottom of the pyramid who lifts everyone else up. The manager is a servant, a coach, and a mentor whose goal is twofold: First managers must help make sure that employees actually want to show up to work, and second managers should help make their employees more successful than they are. When I look at all the most successful organizations that I analyzed in this book, the one thing they all have in common when it comes to management is an enormous amount of trust in making sure their managers are helping create an amazing employee experience.

Internet radio company Pandora is one of the best examples of this. Music is a very personalized thing, so it's natural that Pandora takes the concept of personalized experiences quite seriously and does this by relying heavily on managers. Because the company is publicly traded, there are, of course, some standard HR policies and rules that are put into place around things such as compensation, vacation time, and the like. But outside of these traditional things, the managers are responsible for shaping and creating the experiences for over 2,300 employees.

All employees have their own agreements with their managers on how they prefer to work and what they expect and need to get their jobs done. These aren't driven by blanket policies or rules that every employee has to follow. To be able to create personalized experiences, all the managers at Pandora go through a training program that includes modules that focus on self-awareness and emotional intelligence. The rationale for doing this is that before you can lead others, you must first know more about yourself. Only then can managers at Pandora lead with humility, empathy, and an awareness of what their personal biases might be.

For example, managers at many organizations would typically see going out to happy hour as a kind of team building and bonding activity. However, what if you work in a team with a Type A personality (outgoing, ambitious, competitive, and perhaps impatient) project manager, an introverted software developer, and a very extroverted sales professional? Clearly going out drinking might not make sense here. At organizations like Pandora, managers are trained to see things through the eyes of their team members and then act accordingly. This is what allows the managers to do things such as treat people fairly, help foster a sense of purpose, make others feel valued, and the like. The leaders at Pandora genuinely understand their employees individually, so they know what they care about and what they value.

CHAMPIONED BY EVERYONE

As I mentioned at the start of the book, the overlap between employee needs, wants, and expectations, and the organizational design of those employee needs, wants, and expectations is where employee experience is created. This means that every employee from the intern to the CEO needs to get into the habit of sharing, collaborating, and providing feedback around what they want their work experience to look like.

Looking at this framework I want to stress a few key points. Although the people team inside of your organization may be responsible for helping guide everyone else, this concept of employee experience needs to be embedded everywhere and practiced by everyone. Think of employee experience as the sun, and the rest of your company rotates around it.

CHAPTER 23

A Lesson from Airbnb

Every organization has a different purpose, culture, mix of employees, business model, and priorities. This is why I caution readers to create something that makes sense for your organization instead of trying to copy what someone else is doing. Although this can be tempting to do, it will end up hurting you in the long run.

One of the organizations that have pioneered employee experience is Airbnb. Mark Levy was hired three years ago as the global head of employee experience, and in 2015 Airbnb won Glassdoor's award for being the number one company to work for in America. At Airbnb employee experience refers to the activities, programs, resources, and approaches taken to make sure that employees are set up to be their best selves, feel they belong, and contribute to the success of the company mission and business results.

Three years ago you would be hard-pressed to find many people with *employee experience* in their job titles let alone having an executive with this title. Mark was one of the first executives at a global organization to formally hold this role. When he joined the company one group ran talent, another team handled recruiting, and a third group ran something called *ground control*, which included the workspace environment, internal communications, employee events, and recognition and celebration. All of these functions reported to different people. Airbnb wanted to bring all of these into one function that was ultimately responsible for helping support employees. Airbnb has a rocking customer experience team, so it decided it would make sense to create an employee experience team as well. Originally Mark was responsible for talent (human resources) business partners, talent operations, total rewards, talent programs, compensation and benefits, recruiting, diversity and belonging (its approach to inclusion), learning and organizational development, workplace (facilities, safety and security, food and environments), and ground control, plus any traditional human resources (HR) functions that typically exist inside of an organization. At one point talent information systems and global citizenship were also part of employee experience, but they have since broadened their scope and now reside in other functions. Basically every aspect of how Airbnb touches a prospective, current, or past employee was a part of the employee experience program. It all rolled up to Mark.

When other organizations first found out about how Airbnb was doing things around employee experience, they became quite fascinated with it, and some even attempted to emulate it. But, this is a great example of why you shouldn't copy another organization. What few people know is that Airbnb has since changed its structure around employee experience. According to Mark:

> After 2.5 years of growing the company, expanding the various functions within employee experience, and curating our culture to be recognized as the best place to work by Glassdoor at the end of 2015, it became apparent that pulling all of these groups together to look after the entire employee journey makes a lot of sense. It was also clear that it was impossible for me to be able to go deep into any given area with the responsibility of nine or so distinct functions. In hindsight, the structure of having more integration between the traditional HR functions would have ensured that this group within employee experience would have been more effective rather than leading them all as separate groups within the broader employee experience team.
>
> As such, we are moving to a model where I will be responsible for the workplace and ground control teams. We are looking

for someone else to lead and better integrate the more traditional HR functions like talent business partners, talent operations, talent programs, total rewards, and potentially learning, recruiting, and diversity. The employee experience approach is the right one, though it includes a lot of pieces and parts, which is why it will be great to have someone leading most of the organization while I stay focused on what has made us unique and special all these years.

What we can learn from the Airbnb example is that having one person responsible for literally everything that touches the employees can be too much.

CHAPTER 24

The Role of Employees

If you look at the employee experience design loop, which was discussed earlier in Chapter 15, you will recall that half of it is devoted to employees, which means employees are just as accountable for creating their experiences as the organization is. Although it's tempting to think that the organization should do all the work, this isn't about creating Pinocchio's island where employees can simply ask for and expect to get anything they want. That is not the type of organization that anyone should try to create.

The role of employees starts by making sure they handle their due diligence before starting work at any organization. Remember the company controls the environment, but most of the time the choice of work is up to you. This doesn't mean you have to panic and worry about picking the right career and the right company from day one. That rarely happens. There's nothing wrong with experimenting and searching for a path that makes sense for you. I dabbled in search engine optimization, marketing, strategy consulting, and running my own start-up before I finally found something that I was committed to, and even that may change in the future. My original plan was to work for a few years after college, go back and get my MBA, and then climb the corporate ladder of whatever organization I was working at. I was lying to myself and as a result I made poor choices in employers. Your most important job is simply to be true to yourself. How to do all of this falls outside of the scope of this book, but I can tell you what I did. I tried a bunch of different things until I found what I'm doing now.

Once you discover the work you want to do and the company you want to be a part of, the next step is actually to speak up inside of your organization. This means not only participating in the programs and initiatives that the organization deploys but also providing feedback, ideas, and suggestions to help influence the design of those programs.

If employees don't speak up and participate, then they don't have much of a say when it comes to shaping what their experiences actually look like. I encourage employees to volunteer for beta programs, participate in employee surveys, have discussions with managers, join in focus groups, and speak up at work. Employee experience should not be a one-sided effort; it simply won't be effective.

CHAPTER 25

Where to Start

Many people reading this book are doing so because they want to help redesign their organizations to focus on employee experiences. For me, it's quite clear that this isn't an option; it's the only option. The future of work is about completely redesigning our organizations to put employee experience at the very center of how they operate. The journey is not easy but the rewards along the way are great. As I have tried to make abundantly clear, everything in this book isn't meant to be thought of a checklist. Remember, it's not so much about what your organization does as it is about how your organization does it. So how can you go about creating an organization that is able to deliver on three environments and 17 variables in an amazing way? How can you create an Experiential Organization?

YOU HAVE TO CARE, REALLY CARE

This book acts as a guide for organizations looking to create employee experiences, but it cannot teach you or your leaders to genuinely care about the people who work there. In fact, I don't believe this is something that can be taught. If you, your managers, or your executives do not care about the employees or the team members you work with, then this entire book will be completely useless. This is one of the key distinctions between the truly Experiential Organizations and everyone else. They don't invest in employee experiences for the business value. They invest in them because they care, and the business value comes as a result.

This might sound a bit corny, but have you ever tried to replicate a recipe that a family member perfected? It doesn't quite come out the same. When you ask him or her (typically a grandmother or grandfather) why his or her dish tastes better even though you followed the recipe exactly, he or she typically responds with "because it was made with love." It's not just about what you do or about what you make. It's how you do it. I cannot stress this point enough. What does caring actually look like?

Barry-Wehmiller is a global supplier of manufacturing technology and services with over 11,000 employees. During the 2008 recession it, like many other companies, was forced to make a very difficult decision: sacrifice (lay off) people for the success of the organization. Bob Chapman is the CEO of Barry-Wehmiller and he described the painful decision he was being forced to make. However, Bob isn't an ordinary CEO and Barry-Wehmiller is no ordinary company. This is an organization that genuinely cares about its people, so much so that it even measures divorce rates and the "hearts" of team members. Bob thought of his organization as a family, so his thought was "What would a family do if someone were struggling?" Usually, the other family members will come together to contribute resources to help get him or her back on his or her feet. With this concept in mind Bob decided to try a bold idea. Instead of laying anyone off from the company, what if everyone just took a month off work? This way everyone kept his or her job, but they all took a bit of a cut. All of the team members embraced this idea. Some even volunteered to take off more time because they were more financially comfortable. The entire organization came together to support one another.

This is what it means to genuinely care about the people who work at your organization. It's about truly understanding and appreciating the impact that your organization has on people's lives, both inside and outside of work.

DEFINE A REASON FOR BEING

The foundation of creating an organization that puts employee experience at its center is creating a Reason for Being that:

1. Focuses on the impact to the world and people
2. Is not centered on financial gain
3. Is something unattainable
4. Rallies employees

The Reason for Being wasn't something that I looked at as binary yes or no question. Instead it was evaluated on a 5-point scale. Out of all of the 252 organizations analyzed in this book, the average score was a 2.16/5, or roughly 43 percent, a staggeringly low score. Some of the organizations with a perfect score on this include Cisco, Airbnb, Facebook, and Google. Organizations that scored 0 on the Reason for Being include PepsiCo, FedEx, and ExxonMobil.

Google's Reason for Being is "to organize the world's information and make it universally accessible and useful." In *Work Rules!* Laszlo Bock wrote, "This kind of a mission gives individuals' work meaning, because it is a moral rather than a business goal."[1]

Everything the organization does and stands for can and should be traced back to the Reason for Being. This includes the values that are created, the way the workspaces are designed, how employees work, the tools that employees use, and how managers lead their teams. This is just as important for start-ups as it is for large global organizations. Oftentimes the senior executives decide on what the Reason for Being of the organization is. However, I encourage you to bring your employees into this process and get their feedback and perspectives on how they would enact the four qualities above. As organizations evolve and adapt and as business models change, the Reason for Being can be adjusted as well.

BUILD A PEOPLE ANALYTICS FUNCTION

The goal of people analytics is to help organizations make better informed decisions based on data and research. This is very much an exciting and growing practice area inside many organizations around the world, some of which still have all of their employee data stored in Excel spreadsheets!

Each organization has its own approach to people analytics, including what the team does, how large the team is, what its priorities are, and how the team is structured. David Green, the global director of people analytics solutions at IBM Kenexa Smarter Workforce, has done an amazing job of compiling stories and examples that he has been sharing on his LinkedIn page, which I encourage you to check out. Many of the stories and examples in this section come from David's interviews and from the introductions he has made for me to various people analytics teams. Although many great case studies, stories, and people analytics examples exist, they are all rather unique. Still, there are some common attributes that the most successful people analytics teams share.

Start Small

Remember that many of the organizations like IBM, Cisco, and Microsoft have been in the people analytics game for a few years now, but even these teams had to start somewhere. Start with the basics, such as looking at any existing employee data you might have, including surveys, compensation and performance data, and tenure. See what insights and what advice or action items you might be able to share with various business units. Just by looking at these data points, you might be able to identify the relationship between pay and performance, the relationship between performance and tenure, and which teams are the highest performing. Ask a few basic questions, such as:

- What's the average tenure of employees?
- Which teams perform the best?
- How large is each team?

- Do people who get paid more stay longer?
- Do people with more senior job titles stay longer?

If you recall, one of the best ways to create employee experiences is by knowing your people and that starts with people analytics. Everything you do and all the data you look at should be centered on knowing your workforce better. This team is typically composed of data scientists, visualization specialists, engineers, and other very smart people who understand how to collect, analyze, visualize, and interpret data. It's common to find several PhDs on people analytics teams. This function also needs to work with the various lines of business to understand their challenges and potential solutions.

I recently spoke with Alexis Fink, who is the general manager, talent intelligence and analytics at Intel Corporation, which has around 100,000 employees. Her people analytics team comprises 25 really smart individuals. She had some great advice for organizations looking to begin their people analytics journey.

The first thing organizations should do is to start with what she calls "the what questions." These are basic questions about composition and patterns in your workforce, such as "What is the average team size?" "What's the diversity of our workforce?" "What is the average tenure?" These are basic questions that organizations should be able to answer based on data they already collect. If your organization isn't collecting any data, well, then you have much bigger things to worry about!

Once basic data is in place, the next step is to look at the "why questions." Examples of these are "Why is one group more successful than another?" "Why are the high-performing managers doing things differently?" "Why does this group of employees have more internal movement than a comparison group?"

Ideally, organizations can then look at predictive questions. These include "Employees with these attributes are more likely to leave—what we can do to stop that?" or "What are the factors that are driving effective team performance, and what can the organization do to affect that?" This level is where the ability to foresee and even change the path of your labor force comes into play!

These three question layers can be thought of as a type of maturity model. Start with "the what questions" and work your way up.

Identify the Required Skills

According to an article that David Green wrote called "The HR [human resources] Analytics journey at Shell," the 100,000-person oil and gas company focused its capabilities and skills on six areas (taken verbatim from the article):

1. Data Science and Statistics: data cleaning, merging and modelling
2. HR Practice, Policies and Procedures: best practice and Shell specific
3. Business Understanding: what is employee performance and what is the impact of employees on particular business results
4. Consulting: Effective communication/storytelling and building analytics capabilities
5. Assessments/Psychometrics: Design, validation and evaluation of behavioral assessments
6. Employee Surveys: Design and evaluation of employee surveys[2]

Dawn Klinghoffer is the general manager of the HR business insights team at Microsoft (one of the Experiential Organizations). In another great article by David Green called, "The HR Analytics Journey at Microsoft," Dawn shared how they structure their people analytics efforts. The HRBI (Human Resources Business Insights) organization is made up of four teams (again taken verbatim from the article), which are:

1. Workforce Data Insights—this team is focused on providing analytics and reporting to the HR Line organizations supporting our businesses. Typical skill sets include: MBAs with consulting and business analytics skills.
2. Workforce Data Programs—a team providing analytics, measurement and reporting for our COEs [Centers of Excellence] and

the programs that they run. Skill sets: Program managers with experiences in business analytics as well as MBAs.

3. Workforce Data Solutions—this team owns our analytics and reporting tools & technology, and comprises team members with more of a technical background—Skill sets: experience in IT and/or program management on the technical side.

4. Advanced Analytics & Research—this team specializes in advanced analytics & research and comprises skill sets such as industrial/ organizational psychology, statisticians, and mathematicians.[3]

According to Klinghoffer organizations should start with something that is very doable and beneficial, such as looking at attrition. This can be broken down by certain locations, functions, teams, seniority levels, and the like. Exit surveys can be conducted to help provide data for attrition.

Alexis from Intel identified three core groups of skills that organizations should look for:

1. HR domain knowledge—understanding things such as the recruiting process, job structuring, compensation, and leadership and management advancement approaches

2. Analytics mastery—true expertise with numbers, analysis, and data sets. Oftentimes these people have higher education degrees, such as PhDs. Data visualization is also a crucial skill, but oftentimes those who are good at analytics are also good at data visualization.

3. Data management expertise—ability to know how to access, compile, clean, manage, and organize data in a meaningful and usable way.

Oftentimes three different people possess these three skills. Chances are your organization already has these people in house. It's just a matter of bringing them together.

A lot of the success of people analytics depends on making sure that humans are filling out the right information, completely, accurately, consistently, and in a standardized way. Depending on how well your organization has been doing on this front, it can take weeks or years before the people analytics function can provide valuable insights.

Have Executive Support, Typically the Chief People Officer

Every people analytics team I have spoken with has mentioned this as being a crucial factor for long-term success. In most organizations the people analytics function actually sits within HR (or whatever the people function at your organization is called). Ideally, you will have the support of many executives from different business units who all see the value of people analytics. After all, even though this function might sit within HR, the data and insight can be applied across the entire organization. Executive support helps ensure resources are being allocated, expectations are being managed, and decisions are being pushed through.

Alexis also pointed out a few other areas of consideration when looking to garner support. It's important to remember that in many organizations, the primary currency of HR has always been relationships, intuition, guidance, and what many would consider to be soft skills. Some might view a shift toward analytics as something that can threaten their jobs because it has the potential to eliminate the need for those soft skills. It's important to manage this relationship and help team members understand that both soft skills and data are vital and must work together. Last, people analytics teams should learn to build a strong relationship with legal teams because labor and employment laws are quite strict, and not everything that the people analytics team is able to do is considered legal. It's important to understand where these lines are drawn.

Train the Organization

People analytics is still very much an emerging area of practice, which means that the majority of employees inside of your organization might not know what this team does, how to leverage its skills, or even what questions to start asking. As Henry Ford famously said, "If I had asked people what they wanted, they would have said faster horses." It's helpful to provide guidance to the organization on what the purpose of this team is and how other departments and functions can leverage the skills of the people analytics team. This will help them understand how to ask the right questions.

Tell Stories

Most data and analytics teams comprise some very smart people with PhDs. Although the work they do is fascinating and valuable, it's quite useless if the right people aren't able to understand the insight in a meaningful way. Imagine a people analytics team is presenting what they learned about a particular marketing team to the leader of that division. If they show off their calculations, the models they used, and what the findings of their analysis were, then the marketing leader probably won't take much action. However, if this same people analytics team is able to create a narrative around what the data means, then chances are much higher that the marketing team will take action.

BUILD OR IMPROVE THE EXPERIENCE TEAM

Let's face it; HR used to be boring, outdated, and inspiring. I know it's hard to hear but it's true.

That's because this function was traditionally responsible for things such as hiring, firing, compensation, talent acquisition, and governance. Although these things were and continue to be important, they aren't exactly innovating how work gets done, and they are certainly not focused on employee experience. However, today we're starting to see a new HR that is virtually an unrecognizable function. In fact, the very name and title of HR are starting to disappear and are getting replaced by more human-centric roles and names, such as people, talent, and experience departments. This people-centric aspect of the organization is becoming a core component of how work gets done, and sitting at the very center of everything is employee experience. Of course, this isn't about just changing the title of HR leaders. It's about getting them to think and act differently.

Although many of the traditional components of HR still do exist, this group of professionals is now on the very forefront of exploring what the future of work is going to look like. HR is responsible for figuring out how to create an organization where people want to show up to work. This is a very exciting and unique challenge and opportunity.

Everything that I explored in this book is something that HR teams around the world are going to be tasked with guiding, but the organization as a whole will be tasked with implementing it. The role of HR has morphed into organizational design and innovation that has to look at the technologies employees use to work, the spaces in which they work, and the culture employees are surrounded by.

BMC Software has over 6,000 employees around the world, and it is one of the few organizations that has a chief employee experience officer. Her name is Monika Fahlbusch. I spoke with at length with Monika to understand how her role and the HR function are evolving to focus on employee experience. BMC Software used to have a chief human resources officer, but as many other forward-thinking organizations have realized, both that function and the naming of that function have worn out their welcome. Monika and her team wanted to create something that better reflected what this new role and function was really about, employee experience. BMC Software, like many other organizations, has a customer experience team, but rarely do organizations apply this same approach or mentality to look inward at employees.

According to Monika HR needs to have an innovative mind-set that goes beyond traditional HR policies. HR professionals must be the agents of change, creative thought leaders, and the spokespeople for the employees they support. This is what prompted BMC Software to make what many would consider radical changes.

Monika owns all of HR, facilities and real estate, employee communications, community (external giving), and even IT! All of these things fit quite nicely into the three employee experience environments explored in this book. Out of all the organizations I have researched and spoken with, this has been the only instance where I have heard of IT reporting to HR. According to Monika, this new organization that we are going to see will be designed using data and stories. It's going to be up to HR (or whatever this team will be called) to ask, listen, and act on this information.

Google's People Operations team comprises one-third traditional HR practitioners, one-third consultants from top-tier strategy consultancies, and one-third analytically minded professionals who have at least a master's degree in something such as organizational psychology, mathematics, or physics. This approach may or may not work for you, but it has certainly worked for Google.

Figure 25.1 shows how the role of traditional HR is evolving.

Regardless of how you decide to structure employee experience at your organization, the main point is that this a new and emerging role whose purpose is to create a place where people genuinely want to show up to work by focusing on culture, technology, and the physical workspace. This isn't simply about changing the name of the HR function to *employee experience*. All the factors and variables discussed in this book must become a part of your team's arsenal.

DEPLOY FEEDBACK TOOLS/MECHANISMS

Every one of the Experiential Organizations listed in this book has thorough feedback mechanisms that connect the voice of the employee to the decisions that the organization makes. Without this bridge there is no such thing as employee experience. The goal is to create the employee experience design loop, which was discussed earlier in this book where I looked at how General Electric (GE) and Airbnb were implementing this kind of process. Feedback in an organization can happen in only two ways: in person or through technology.

In-Person Feedback

Perhaps the largest area of impact where organizations are seeing the implementation of feedback mechanisms is during the annual performance review. Organizations such as Adobe, T-Mobile, Cisco, and others have made a dramatic shift away from this framework to instead focus on more real-time conversations that happen regularly. In these oftentimes informal discussions leaders are encouraged to not only get to know their people on a professional level but also inquire about their aspirations, goals, and dreams. These open and candid conversations allow managers and executives to better make decisions that affect their people.

PAST	FUTURE
REMOVES LEGALESE, IS HUMAN, AND "THINKS LIKE MARKETING"	REMOVING LEGALESE, BEING HUMAN, AND "THINKING LIKE MARKETING"
HIRED AND FIRED	ENABLES, EMPOWERS, ENGAGES, & CREATES EXPERIENCES
THE "POLICE" OF THE ORGANIZATION	THE COACHES, MENTORS, AND THOUGHT LEADERS OF THE ORGANIZATION
MAINTAINED STATUS QUO	DESTROYS STATUS QUO
NOT TECHNOLOGICALLY ADVANCED	RELIES HEAVILY ON TECHNOLOGY, SUCH AS BIG DATA & ANALYTICS
DIDN'T DEFINE AND LEAD STRATEGY	SHAPES AND LEADS STRATEGY
NO SEAT AT THE TABLE	KEY SEAT AT THE TABLE
PAYROLL, COMPENSATION, & BENEFITS	EMPLOYEE EXPERIENCE
COST CENTER	PROFIT-ENABLING CENTER
CLEARLY DEFINED WORKFORCE	DYNAMIC AND CHANGING WORKFORCE
FOCUSED ON EMPLOYEE INPUTS	FOCUSED ON EMPLOYEE OUTPUTS
TREATED EMPLOYEES LIKE "RESOURCES"	TREATS EMPLOYEES LIKE WATER AND AIR (CAN'T LIVE WITHOUT THEM)
PERFORMANCE APPRAISALS	REAL-TIME RECOGNITION & FEEDBACK WITH EMPLOYEE CHECK-INS
FILLED GAPS IN JOBS	UNLOCKS HUMAN POTENTIAL
ONE-SIZE-FITS-ALL MODEL ACROSS THE ORGANIZATION	ONE-SIZE-BREAKS-ALL APPROACH ACROSS THE ORGANIZATION
SILOED FROM LINES OF BUSINESS	WORKS CLOSELY TO UNDERSTAND BUSINESS NEEDS
MULTIYEAR PROJECT DESIGN AND ROLLOUTS	FAST DESIGN, IMPLEMENTATION, AND ITERATION
HUMAN RESOURCE JOB TITLES	PEOPLE, TALENT, & EXPERIENCE TITLES

JACOB MORGAN
© thefutureorganization.com

FIGURE 25.1 Evolution of HR

Feedback via Technology

As we saw in the GE example earlier, technology is a powerful mechanism for creating a real-time communication, collaboration, and feedback system. For the past few years we have seen organizations around the world invest heavily in internal social networks, custom-built apps, videoconferencing solutions, and other technologies that allow employees to stay connected to one another and information anywhere, anytime, and on any device. Creating this type of connected organization means that feedback can be provided in real time from anyone.

BMC Software does an outstanding job of this with several technologies it deployed and built (based on employee feedback). These include a new employee intranet built from the ground up and shifting away from traditional unified communications solutions to a more mobile friendly and modern workforce. Along with some other technology enhancements, employees at BMC Software are able to provide feedback to one another anywhere, anytime, and on any device, creating a truly mobile workforce.

In August of 2015 the *New York Times* published a rather scathing article by Jodi Kantor and David Streitfeld about Amazon called "Inside Amazon: Wrestling Big Ideas in a Bruising Workplace," which made it sound like the company is one of the world's worst places to work. A handful of employees were used as sources for the article. I found that quite interesting because Amazon is one of the Experiential Organizations that scored exceptionally high in areas such as having a physical space that reflects the values of the organization, diversity and inclusion, and having a sense of purpose. However, Amazon also scored poor (for an Experiential Organization) in areas such as having managers who act as coaches and mentors and investing in the well-being of employees, both of which were huge points of contention in the *New York Times* article.

After this article was published Amazon made several changes, and perhaps the most impactful is the introduction and the widespread scale of Amazon Connections, an internal system used to collect employee feedback. Originally this was used just for blue-collar workers but has since been rolled out to white-collar workers as well. According to a Bloomberg article by Spencer Soper, "Amazon Wants to Know How Its Employees Feel Every Day," "Dubbed Amazon Connections, the internal system poses questions daily to employees to collect responses on topics such as job satisfaction, leadership and training opportunities." Teams then compile and analyze the feedback into daily reports, which are shared with Amazon.[4] This is certainly a noble effort by the company to make sure that it is constantly focusing on creating great employee experiences. Not coincidentally, all the factors mentioned in the Bloomberg article are also part of the 17 employee experience variables discussed in this book.

IMPLEMENT COOL SPACES, ACE TECHNOLOGY, AND CELEBRATED CULTURE

Through people analytics and feedback mechanisms, your organization should get a very solid sense of what your employees care about and why. This foundation is what will allow you to go from using the 17 variables above as a checklist to using them as a framework to create amazing employee experiences. Depending on how aggressive you want to be, you can tackle as many of these simultaneously as you want. In fact some of them actually go hand in hand.

Technological Environment

Consumer grade technology: Deploy technologies that are modern, beautiful, and useful. Stay away from legacy systems.

Available to everyone: Give everyone access to every technology (hardware and software) whenever and wherever possible.

Focused on employee needs: Understand how and why employees work before giving them tools your organization thinks they need. Talk to them, interview them, and observe them.

Physical Environment

Workspace options: Forget about open or closed spaces. Create multiple workspaces based on how employees work. Give them choice.

Values reflected in the workspace: Avoid having your values seen as lip service. Try to create physical manifestations of your values in the workplace.

Being proud to bring in friends or visitors: Allow friends, visitors, and strangers to tour your spaces. If you aren't ready to do this, then revamp your workspace! Your workspaces are employee experience centers.

Workplace flexibility and autonomy: Focus on inputs, not outputs. Implement flexible work programs and treat your people like adults. Let them have autonomy and flexibility but also the accountability that comes with them. Work-life balance has become work-life integration.

Cultural Environment

Sense of purpose: Show employees the impact they are having on customers, the community, and the world. Make the connection between work and impact by telling and sharing stories.

Fair treatment: Teach employees about biases and how to avoid them. Provide open communication channels for employees to share concerns or issues without judgment or penalty. Create employee committees to help ensure fair treatment.

Feeling valued: Listen and acknowledge employees and make changes to the organization based on their feedback. Provide adequate compensation and benefits. Recognize employees for the hard work they do by creating special programs around this.

Managers acting like coaches and mentors: Get rid of the old stereotypical manager mentality. Hire and train managers to focus on the success of their people. Create ongoing and open conversations about work and life between employees.

Feeling like you're part of a team: Acknowledge team, not just individual, performance. Create communities of passion and of interest. Allow employees to share their stories and experience with one another and with the world.

Ability to learn something new and advance and get the resources to do so: Give employees access to multiple learning resources whether they be proprietary or third party. Understand what employees want and need when they talk about advancement.

Referring others: Most organizations in the world have referral programs, but simply giving employees money won't get you more candidates. Focus on the employee experience, and others will refer prospects because they want to, not because they are being paid to do so.

Diversity and inclusion: Partner with third-party organizations that focus on diversity and inclusion, and make this an initiative that is tied to executive compensation. Create internal groups and committees around various diversity and inclusion efforts. Adjust hiring approaches if needed.

Health and wellness: Invest in the whole employee, not just the physical or mental aspect. This means going beyond just a gym and healthy food options. Do your best to take care of your people.

Brand perception: Share stories of the impact your organization is having on employees and the community. Participate in the various lists and rankings that rank and highlight exceptional organizations. Strive to be an ethical organization that positively affects all those who come in contact with it.

EXAMPLE: ADOBE

Adobe is one the Experiential Organizations that I researched for this book, and here's what it is doing for each one of the 17 variables, sometimes quoted directly from its website.[5]

Technological Environment

Consumer Grade Technology

- Employees are offered a variety of laptops, tablets, monitors, Adobe software, and so on and can select the technologies that work best for them and their job function.
- They also have access to Adobe software, which is built with the consumer grade mind-set.

Available to Everyone

- All of the 15,000+ employees at Adobe have access to Adobe's creative software and a 24/7 digital learning environment where they can learn professional skills anywhere and anytime.

Focused on Employee Needs

- In addition to the modern software, hardware, and device options that employees have at their disposal, they have access to workspaces with state-of-the-art videoconferencing, interactive whiteboards, and a robust intranet platform where employees have access to real-time company information, development resources, and tools they need to be effective in their roles.
- All of these things are based on what employees need and want to be successful at work.

Physical Environment

Workspace Options

- The spaces at Adobe are modern and vibrant, with a largely open floor plan. There are also plenty of communal areas and alternative workspaces, such as cafes, telephone booths, outside patios, conference rooms, and other community spaces.

Values Reflected in the Workspace

- The core values at Adobe are "Genuine, Exceptional, Innovative & Involved."
- Adobe has completely redesigned its 143,000-square-feet headquarters in the Bay Area to include a modern and innovative vibe, which includes a game area, a gym, meditation spaces, and even an artisan sandwich shop.
- Adobe has a program called Kickbox where any employee is able to get access to a $1,000 prepaid credit card and an innovation workshop to come up with a new idea or concept.
- The mainly open floor plan, gorgeous new design, Kickbox program, implementation of the enhanced workplace technologies, and investments in the community and diversity all help make the Adobe values come to life.

Being Proud to Bring in Friends or Visitors

- Adobe sites in San Jose, San Francisco, Seattle, and Lehi offer an annual Adobe Field Trip once a year where employees bring family to work to participate in a variety of fun activities.
- Adobe regularly hosts tours for students, and employees are able to bring in friends for a tour pretty much anytime they want.

Workplace Flexibility and Autonomy

- The working relationships are owned and defined by the employee and manager. Together they determine the flexibility and autonomy needs. There's no official company-wide policy that everyone must follow.
- Adobe is also piloting a flexibility plan for employees who are returning from a lengthy leave to ease back into work (for example, from maternity leave).

Cultural Environment

Sense of Purpose

- Adobe measures purpose (as it defines it). In fact, 91 percent of employees believe that Adobe and its products have a positive impact on society.
- Adobe works hard to help foster a sense of purpose in three ways:
  - Provide rich volunteer opportunities
  - Connect employees directly to the customer experience
  - Create a sense of pride in Adobe as a company
- Adobe makes sure it hires people who have a genuine interest and drive to change the world and affect communities positively.
- Leadership capability training is also available for all employees at every level to help them accelerate and grow their careers.

Fair Treatment

- Adobe has several networks, including AccessAdobe, AdobeProud (LGBTQ), Adobe & Women, Asian Employee Network, Black Employee Network, Hispanic & Latino Employee Network, and Veterans Employee Network, to "help foster an inclusive work environment."

- It received a perfect score and the recognition of being a Best Place to Work for LGBTQ Equality on the Human Rights Campaign's Corporate Equality Index.
- Adobe partners "with Stanford University's Clayman Institute for Gender Research as well as Catalyst to access resources, research, events and a community of diversity and inclusion leaders."

Feeling Valued

- For careers, Adobe developed a learning environment that fosters a learning culture that includes a leadership development program for all employees and access to real-time skills development through a digital learning platform. In addition, Adobe offers an educational reimbursement program of $10,000 per year to help employees who want to pursue further education.
- Employees are recognized for their innovation, and commitment to customers and one another, through various awards, such as Founder's Awards and team awards.
- Adobe has great wellness and financial benefits for employees and their loved ones.
- Various community celebration events are held throughout the year for employees.
- Adobe does company check-in surveys (it was one of the first major companies to abolish annual reviews). Each employee receives a survey once a year, but not everyone will take it at the same time. There are four survey periods per year, and employees are randomly selected to take it during one of the assigned periods. Adobe then gets the feedback and modifies whatever is needed.

Managers Acting like Coaches and Mentors

- Adobe offers several programs to encourage mentorship and coaching.
- "Development programs for female employees include the Women's Executive Shadow Program, Worldwide Field Operations Leadership Circles, Voice & Influence Circles and WOMEN Unlimited," along with an annual women's summit.

- A yearlong Campus to Adobe Life development program is available for hires right out of a university. Throughout the first calendar year of joining Adobe, university hires are automatically enrolled. This program is designed to complement the comprehensive onboarding and integration plan managers have for their employees. The Campus to Adobe Life program includes regular one-on-one sessions with a professionally trained Co-Active coach and events for socializing, networking, and building business acumen.
- Adobe managers have a genuine interest in the success of their people and provide individual coaching and mentoring to employees.

Feeling like You're Part of a Team

- Adobe Life is a behind-the-scenes look of what it's like to work at the company. This program features tweets from employees, a magazine (which highlights everything from outstanding employees to community involvement efforts), and photos.
- By creating all these communities and sharing the content about them, employees very much feel like they are a part of a team.

Ability to Learn Something New and Advance and Get the Resources to Do So

- All employees are encouraged to become learn-it-alls.
- Adobe has a dedicated page on its intranet that curates learning opportunities to amplify skills and offers learning resources from its Leading@Adobe program and external resources, such as Lynda.com, Harvard ManageMentor, Safari, getAbstract, and its Goldmine Research Portal.
- Employees are offered memberships to Catalyst (the leading nonprofit organization with a mission to accelerate progress for women through workplace inclusion), and Aperian Global (learning resource for individuals and teams to perform effectively worldwide).
- Employees also receive discounts if they'd like to pursue learning with General Assembly, Udemy, or Udacity.
- Adobe offers lateral moves into different business units to advance skills or offers promotions to more senior roles.

- For fiscal year 2016 year to date, 22 percent of filled positions at Adobe were from internal transfers. Year to date approximately 15 percent of Adobe's employees were promoted.

Referring Others

- Although Adobe does offer a referral bonus of $2,000 in the United States, this amount varies by country. It specifically looks for high-performing individuals who can help advance Adobe's industry leadership and people who reinforce the company's values: "Genuine, Exceptional, Innovative & Involved."
- Employees can submit the resumes of people they'd like to refer directly to their hiring manager and a recruiter along with a note that explains why their referral would be a great addition to Adobe.
- The employee referral rate is between 25 percent and 30 percent.

Diversity and Inclusion

- In July 2016 Adobe released equal pay data for the U.S. workforce, and in 2015, it strengthened its family leave policies for employees in the United States, India, and Australia.
- Adobe is "working to diversify the tech industry through our Youth Coding Initiative, GenHERation sponsorship, GEM [National Consortium for Graduate Degrees for Minorities in Engineering and Science] Fellowship program, and other strategic investments." It partners with organizations such as Girls Who Code, Black Girls Code, CodeNow, Urban Arts Partnership, Technovation, ChickTech, City Year, and Code as a Second Language "to further drive global impact."

Health and Wellness

- Adobe invests in programs to support employees so that they can be at their best every day. Benefits include medical, dental, vision, 401(k) plan, and exchange stock portfolio.
- There's no specified amount of vacation days or paid time off for full-time Adobe employees, and every five years employees earn a sabbatical.

- Big-growth locations provide on-site gyms, and Adobe offers up to $360 per year for gym memberships, bike share memberships, fitness classes, massages, nutritional counseling, financial advice, and much more to help employees and their families maintain a well-rounded, healthy lifestyle.
- Some locations also offer locally sourced foods.

Brand Perception

- Interbrand recently listed Adobe as a top riser and a top-growing brand, ranked number 63 on the list of 100 companies, up five spots from last year. Adobe debuted in 2009 at number 95.
- Adobe is known as an employer of choice around the world—listed on *Fortune's* Best 100 Companies to Work For; Best Place to Work in India, Germany, Australia and the United Kingdom; Best Multinational Place to Work, Most inDemand Employer on LinkedIn; Glassdoor's Best Place to Work; and CareerBliss's Happiest Companies to Work For; *Forbes's* Most Innovative Companies, and others.
- Ranked as an Experiential Organization

Highlighting this list of what Adobe is investing in doesn't even begin to do justice to the immense work that the company has put into employee experience. However, hopefully this will give you a sense of what some of those investments were and continue to be. Like the other Experiential Organizations featured in this book, Adobe genuinely cares about its people and it shows.

IDENTIFY AND CREATE MOMENTS THAT MATTER (OR MOMENTS OF IMPACT)

What are the key moments in the lives of your people? This is the first question that organizations have to answer. Cisco has a great framework it uses for this.

You can see the 11 moments in Figure 25.2.

FIGURE 25.2 Cisco's Our People Deal

Source: Cisco.[6]

Let's look at what these moments that matter actually are:

First Impression: Cisco knows it has only one chance to make a first impression on employees. That's why it's improving the interview, offer, and first day experiences with the intersection of human touch and digital.

My Development: Cisco is upgrading, organizing, and communicating development tools and offerings to help employees continue to learn and grow professionally.

My Leader: Great teams need great leaders. Cisco is developing tools and processes for leaders to understand and lead with their unique strengths. Cisco inspires curiosity to explore how to become a great team leader.

My Personal Experiences: Developing programs that help Cisco deliver the right support for employees experiencing major life events while adapting to regional and cultural needs, including having a baby, planning for college, caring for an elderly parent, or dealing with a family crisis

My Innovation: Empowering every employee to innovate and make a meaningful difference. Cisco is currently focused on its second Innovate Everywhere Challenge and creating a centralized hub for innovation.

My Rewards: Striving to create a meaningful rewards experience—including perks, benefits, pay, and recognition—that encourages productivity, attracts and retains talent, and is one size fits one (personalized).

My Technology: Simplifying, centralizing, and personalizing Cisco's technology solutions—things such as Refresh, eStore, and CEC [Cisco Employee Connection, its internal website]—to help employees be more productive every day.

My Workplace: Cisco is creating a connected workspace that empowers employees to collaborate, innovate, and deliver amazing outcomes for their teams and customers.

My Lasting Impression: Initiatives that foster a positive and respectful transition from Cisco, show appreciation for employees' time with the company, and create an environment for a lifelong relationship through an alumni network.

My Team: Performance lives in teams so Cisco identified what characterizes its best teams and shared tools with its people to bring out the best in their teams—lifting the overall performance of the organization.

My Making a Difference: Cisco is committed to helping employees support causes and the communities they care about, accelerate social change, and invest in a better tomorrow. Cisco is currently doing this by focusing on enhancing volunteering, donations, and corporate social responsibility initiatives.

The framework that Cisco provides here can be a great starting point for any organization. You will notice that Cisco uses all three types of moments that matter: specific, ongoing, and created. For example, First Impression comprises a few very specific moments, such as the interview process and an employee's first day on the job. My Leader addresses the ongoing relationship that an employee has with his or her team. My Innovation allows Cisco to create specific moments, such as innovation jams.

Your organization can start with perhaps two or three moments that matter and then expand from there. Identifying these moments doesn't need to be a complicated or tedious task. Encourage leaders to have one-on-one conversations with employees, hold focus groups at various career stages, conduct a few surveys, and leverage whatever technology solutions you might have to get employees to open up. Have a conversation with your people, and ask them what they care about and why. Leveraging the people analytics team will help identify what these moments actually are and will allow you to easily categorize the moments that matter into one of the three categories I talked about earlier.

THINK OF YOUR ORGANIZATION LIKE A LAB INSTEAD OF A FACTORY

You probably haven't heard of Sir Richard Arkwright, but he was actually quite a well-known inventor and entrepreneur. Arkwright is credited with being the creator of the modern-day factory (his did cotton spinning). This was the first time in modern business when people were reduced to mere replaceable commodities at scale. Factories were behemoths that had more and better resources to produce more product cheaper and so they did quite well. This factory model was then copied all over the world until Henry Ford further revolutionized this concept with mass production via assembly line. Factory jobs were long, hard, monotonous, and repetitive. Organizations that operate like factories see environments where employees adhere to a dress code, work in similar spaces, don't ask questions or share ideas, commute to and from the office to show up and leave at the same time every day, and work in an environment that is routine, repetitive, and focused on maintaining the status quo. Organizations that operate like laboratories are different, as shown in Figure 25.3.

One of the fascinating things about Experiential Organizations is that they view themselves more like laboratories than factories. These

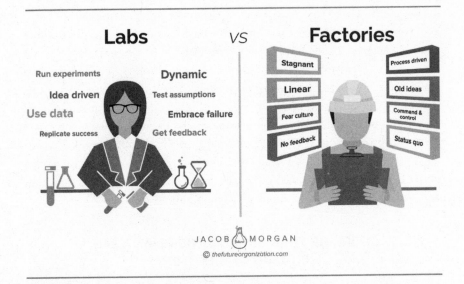

FIGURE 25.3   Key Differences Between Labs and Factories, Labs Will Succeed, Factories Will Not

organizations don't claim to have all the answers or the best solutions to employee experience (or the future of work for that matter). Experiential Organizations embrace failure, rely on data to make decisions, test new ideas, embrace employee feedback, and encourage and support their people. Not only is this simply the right thing to do, but it also serves as a unique business advantage because the best way to mitigate risks or identify opportunities is by experimenting or testing ideas. Airbnb treats its physical space like software where it is constantly testing and implementing new workspace designs to see what works best. Google tested numerous approaches to get employees to eat healthier foods at work before realizing that the best solution was to put the healthy food choices in transparent containers at eye level and the unhealthy options in translucent containers below eye level. Cisco is testing out a new approach to talent that emulates a freelance marketplace inside of the organization. LinkedIn is playing around with the idea of giving employees badges for new skills they earn at work. The list goes on and on. Think of your organization more like a laboratory and less like a factory.

NOTES

1. Bock, Laszlo. *Work Rules! Insights from Inside Google That Will Transform How You Live and Lead*. New York: Grand Central, 2015.
2. https://www.linkedin.com/pulse/hr-analytics-journey-shell-david-green.
3. https://www.linkedin.com/pulse/people-analytics-interviews-3-dawn-klinghoffer-microsoft-green.
4. https://www.bloomberg.com/news/articles/2015-10-09/amazon-asks-corporate-employees-for-feedback-on-work.
5. http://www.adobe.com/diversity.html.
6. Courtesy of Cisco.

CHAPTER 26

Focus on What Makes Your Company Unique

If you were to interview a senior leader at any one of the Experiential Organizations in this book, they would all tell you the same thing. They focus on what makes them unique and don't focus on what other organizations doing. It's good to be aware of what other organizations are doing, but copying them will get you nowhere. It's tempting to copy Google, Amazon, Cisco, or any one of the other Experiential Organizations featured in this book. But doing so would be a mistake.

F5 Networks is a company that you've probably never heard of. They are publicly traded with around 5,000 employees and are in the business of application delivery. Basically if you use the Internet, you've interacted with F5. In 2015 Glassdoor named it as a Best Place to Work, so naturally I was curious to speak with its leaders. I spoke with Rich James, the staffing director, and Wei-Ling Poon, human resources business partner, Southeast Asia, and talent and organization development, Asia Pacific Japan. My mind was boggled when I found out that employees at F5 Networks work in cubicles, most employees commute to and from the office and work 9 to 5, still have annual reviews, and don't have unlimited gourmet meals! How can this possibly be? Most people reading about F5 would say that it is simply behind the times. However, nothing could be farther from the truth. It simply focuses on investing in things that employees care about as opposed to focusing on what other companies are doing. For example, F5 provides employees with challenging work, has social events, has a strong diversity and inclusion program, invests heavily in local communities, and prioritizes a strong work-life balance (at around 5 PM the offices are usually empty). People love the culture, and employees get access to the latest and greatest technologies to get their jobs done. This is what employees care about, and this is what F5 Networks invests in. Organizations like F5 are rare but they do exist. What we can learn from them is that it's crucial to focus on the things that matter to your people.

Facebook is another great example of an organization that doesn't follow conventional trends. Many of the Experiential Organizations (and others) have been getting rid of traditional annual reviews and ratings in favor of something more real time. In fact this has been one of the biggest trends in the HR world. *Harvard Business Review* recently published a great article called "Let's Not Kill Performance Evaluations Yet," which was written with Lori Goler, the head of people at Facebook; Janelle Gale, head of HR business partners at Facebook; and Adam Grant, a professor at Wharton and author of the best-selling book *Originals*. The article stated almost 90 percent of employees at Facebook actually wanted to keep the annual review! Instead of abandoning the annual review, the team at Facebook simply looked for a way to make it better. They did this by introducing things such as peer written evaluations and a team of analysts who examine the evaluations for signs of bias.[1] Facebook did its own research on the annual review, and instead of following the popular "no annual review" trend, it did what made sense for the company and listened to its employees.

As we saw with Amazon, even Experiential Organizations are not perfect. No organization will ever be perfect. Regardless of how hard you try to create the perfect employee experience for everyone, there will always be people who are less than satisfied with working there, but that's okay. Airbnb didn't score that well in employees having the ability to learn something new or advance, Adobe didn't score off the charts in the area of having managers who are coaches and mentors, and neither did Cisco, Google, or Riot Games. Salesforce.com didn't score that high in workplace flexibility and autonomy. The point is that no company scored perfect in every area. Every organization, regardless of how good it is, can improve.

In a letter to shareholders Jeff Bezos, the CEO of Amazon, summed it up nicely: "We never claim that our approach is the right one—just that it's ours—and over the last two decades, we've collected a large group of like-minded people. Folks who find our approach energizing and meaningful." Even organizations like Netflix, a preExperiential organization, are candid in telling prospective employees that their company isn't for everyone. Laszlo Bock, advisor of Google, echoes this statement in *Work Rules!*: "That's not to say we have all the answers. We don't. In fact, we have more questions than answers. But we aspire to bring more insight, innovation, and anticipation to Googlers and how they experience work."[2]

NOTES

1. https://hbr.org/2016/11/lets-not-kill-performance-evaluations-yet.
2. Bock, Laszlo. *Work Rules! Insights from Inside Google That Will Transform How You Live and Lead*. New York: Grand Central, 2015.

CHAPTER 27

Size, Industry, and Location Don't Matter

As you can imagine, it's quite a bit easier to focus on employee experiences if you're a growing company that has to invest actively in culture, new technologies, and physical spaces. Newer companies don't have the baggage of dealing with many of the outdated workplace practices and approaches that plague many of the older and larger organizations around the world. The concept of employee experience applies to any organization regardless of size, industry, or location. Smaller, less established organizations have the benefit of being able to make these changes quicker without having to get rid of older approaches, but on the other hand, these smaller organizations also have fewer resources to work with.

I'll be honest; larger organizations here are going to have a more challenging time, simply because these organizations have more people, which means more bureaucracy, and because they usually have to change many years of doing things. Although some of the Experiential Organizations mentioned in this book are young disruptors, such as Airbnb and Facebook, there are also plenty of larger, more established players that have had to make considerable investments and changes. Consider Microsoft, which was founded in 1975 and has around 115,000 employees around the world, or Apple, which was founded in 1976 and has around 115,000 employees as well.

The size, industry, or location of an organization is not an excuse for not investing in employee experience. It's simply a matter of priority and commitment. Still, I will acknowledge that all the Experiential Organizations can be considered technology companies. It's hard to say whether this is a coincidence or is industry specific. After all there are many other technology companies, such as HP and Ingram Micro, which scored rather poorly. It's becoming harder to differentiate organizations by industry as every company is becoming a technology company. For those that prefer to stick to traditional industry definitions though, rest assured that plenty of nontechnology companies were quite close to becoming Experiential Organizations. Starbucks, Nike, Humana, Capital One, Dow Chemical, St. Jude Children's Research Hospital, Best Buy, Whirlpool, and dozens of others were all ranked as preExperiential, meaning they were in the second-highest category of organizations. I fully expect that over time, we will see more organizations follow what I like to call the path to the Experiential Organization.

As I mentioned earlier in this book, organizations can just as easily fall backward as they can move forward. You can see this in figure 27.1. Any organization can follow the approaches outlined here. But, several specific traits of Experiential Organizations outlined in this book truly set them apart from everyone else.

ALWAYS IMPROVE

As you saw throughout this book, even the Experiential Organizations are flawed. That doesn't keep them from constantly trying to improve. These organizations know the areas they are lacking in, and they are constantly looking for ways to get better. It's okay to admit you are not perfect but always reach for the stars.

THINK LIKE A LABORATORY

As new approaches get introduced and as the discussions about the future of work continue to evolve, the Experiential Organizations evolve.

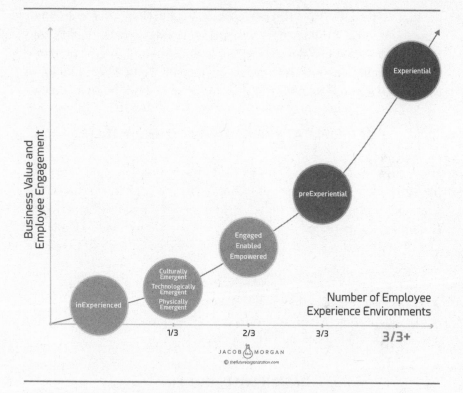

FIGURE 27.1   Path to the Experiential Organization

These companies think of themselves as laboratories that are constantly testing, experimenting, and using data to evolve. Try to break things and then rebuild them where they come out better faster and stronger. Think of the various hackathons that organizations like LinkedIn and T-Mobile host.

MOVE BEYOND CHECKLISTS

I've repeated this numerous times. Any organization can follow the approaches outlined in this book, but simply implementing a program around the 17 variables won't guarantee anything. The variables and environments outlined in this book are simply the things that employees care about most. I did my best to share some frameworks, models, and ideas for how you can design and implement them, but I recommend that you build on this with your own take. Remember, employee experience is not just about what you do but also about how you do it.

PUT PEOPLE AT THE CENTER AND KNOW THEM

If you truly want to be an Experiential Organization, then put your people at the center. Don't just talk about or say how much you care about your employees. Actually do something about employee experience. If employee experience is a priority, then you should make significant investments in this space. Redesign your organization to put people at the center.

Experiential Organizations truly know their people, not just from a people analytics standpoint but also from an individual manager to employee perspective. Employees are viewed as whole people with passions, fears, interests, and aspirations.

DESIGN WITH, NOT FOR

It's tempting to create things for your employees, but the right approach is to create things with them. Be as transparent as you can, and ask for feedback often both via technology and via in-person discussions. Create the employee experience design loop, and bring employees into the experience design process whenever and wherever you can.

CARE

You can't teach this or somehow create a sense of caring. This ultimately stems from the executives running the organization and the managers who are leading the teams. If your leaders don't care about people, actually care, then no amount of effort or investment in employee experience will yield results.

FOCUS ON WHAT MAKES YOU UNIQUE

You've read about dozens of organizations in this book. Some of the examples you will be able to relate to and others you won't. Don't worry about copying anyone else. Use the examples and the stories in this book to focus on what makes you unique, and build on that as much as you can. People work at your company not because you're copying Google or Facebook, but because you are you.

CHAPTER 28

A Futurist's Perspective

I make a living speaking at dozens of conferences each year, advising some of the world's most forward-thinking organizations, providing thought leadership to vendors, and creating content for anyone to access, including podcasts, videos, and articles. As a futurist part of my job isn't to predict the future but to keep people and organizations from being surprised by what the future will bring. Not only do I explore the future of work, but I also look at specific industries ranging from finance to pharmaceutical. Every organization around the world is powered by people and the influx of AI and technology is finally forcing us to consider what a people-centric organization actually looks like.

One evening while writing this book I was watching a show on TV and a commercial came on for a particular drug. At the end of the commercial the side effects were listed—weight gain, nausea, anxiety, difficulty breathing, sleeplessness, hair loss, bleeding from the eyes, skin discoloration, and possibly death. I nearly fell off the couch! Who in their right mind would take a drug like that? Then I thought about it for a moment and realized that most of us work for organizations that have the exact same side effects. Why is it that we aren't willing to take the drug with the scary side effects yet we are willing to subject ourselves to countless hours of working for an organization that has the same results? Save yourself some time, stay home and just take the drug.

Now think about your organization and ask yourself what the side effects of working there are. Do you have anxiety, arguments with your spouse, weight problems, or issues with bleeding eyeballs? Or perhaps you feel inspired, fulfilled, curious, challenged, and supported. Interestingly enough when I have confidential discussions with executives I ask them, "If I could bottle up what it was like to work at your organization and give you that in pill form right now, would you swallow the pill?" Almost always the answer is "no." How can we expect employees to swallow that same pill when the leaders who work there won't? It's time to change that.

As I look at the various trends that affect the future of work—AI and automation, alternative work arrangements, organizational design, changing behaviors, and the like—one thing is resoundingly clear. We are now at a crucial point when organizations must make a choice. Do they redesign themselves to put employees at the center, or do they keep carrying on the way they always have? Focusing on short-term Band-Aid solutions is no longer enough. We need new engines.

All the data that I have compiled and all the companies I have researched clearly show that the business impact of employee experience is great but only if you go all in.

I understand that the task is great and that the decision isn't an easy one to make. Should you really get rid of the decades of older work styles and approaches in favor of this concept of employee experience? Yes, you should. As I look ahead to the coming years, it's quite difficult to imagine a scenario in which an organization can thrive without focusing on employee experience. To reach a higher peak, organizations must first climb down the mountain that they have been traversing. My hope is that this book has given you the inspiration, the guidance, and the tools you need to begin or continue on that journey.

Life is short. We all deserve, and in fact, should demand, to work for an organization that has been (re)designed to truly know its people and has mastered the art and science of creating a place where people want, not need, to show up to work. We all deserve and should demand to be a part of an Experiential Organization. We live in a world of "short-termism" with a focus on quarterly profits which is makes it hard to want to invest in something that can potentially take years to see impact from. What we need now our executives with the commitment to change, managers with the willingness to lead the change, and employees with the courage to speak up to force the change to happen. Are you that executive, that manager, or that employee?

Appendix

Employee Experience Score

1. Your organization offers employees multiple workspace options (e.g., open spaces, conference rooms, quiet areas, collaboration spaces, cafe style environments, etc.).
2. The physical space reflects the values of your organization (e.g., if the values are collaboration, openness, transparency, and fun, then you wouldn't expect to see a dull environment with nothing but cubicles!).
3. You feel proud to bring a friend/visitor to your office.
4. Your organization offers flexible work options (such as the ability to work your own hours wherever you want) and encourages autonomy.
5. You feel a sense of purpose.
6. You feel you are treated fairly.
7. You feel valued.
8. You feel your managers are coaches and mentors.
9. You feel like you are part of a team.
10. If you want to learn something new or advance within your organization, you are given the resources and opportunity to do so.
11. You refer others to work at the organization.
12. You feel that the organization you work for is diverse and inclusive.
13. Your organization invests in employees' well-being (physical and mental health).
14. Generally speaking, your organization has a strong positive brand perception.
15. Generally, the technology that you use in your organization is consumer grade (meaning it's so well designed, useful, and valuable that you would consider using something similar in your personal life if it existed).
16. Generally, the technology is available to everyone at your organization who wants it.

17. Generally, the technology you use in your organization is focused on the needs of the employees instead of just on the technical requirements and specifications of the organization.

These are the 17 questions I used to evaluate the 252 organizations. Each question was scored on a scale of 1 through 5 where 1 means strongly disagree and 5 means strongly agree. The first four questions explore the physical environment, the next ten questions look at the cultural environment, and the final three questions analyze the technological environment. Once you go through and review all 17 questions you can use the following framework to get your score:

Add up your score for the first four questions (e.g., 18) and multiply that total by 0.3 (e.g., 5.4) and then add those two numbers together (e.g. 18 + 5.4 = 23.4). The max score here is 26. Add up your score for the next ten questions and multiply the total score by 0.4, again add the two numbers together. The max score here is 70. Add up your score for the last three questions and multiple that score by 0.3, add those two numbers. The max score here is 19.5. Finally, add up the totals from each of the sections and you will have your employee experience score for a maximum of 115.5. You can look at your total score as well as your score for the cultural, technological, and physical environments. Since various formulas and weights were applied to each environment you can visit TheFutureOrganization.com to get your company's total score, a breakdown of each environment score, the category your organization falls under, and some free guidance and next steps that you can implement as well as additional resources. As a general ballpark, if you scored 80% of above in all three environments you are likely an Experiential Organization. If you averaged between 70%–80% you are either Engaged, Empowered, or Enabled (depending on which environments you scored higher in). Between 60%–70% you are likely an Emergent organization (again depending on which environments you scored highest in). And if you scored below 60% you are an inExperienced organization. Again, to get an accurate breakdown and score, visit TheFutureOrganization.com.

Index

Page references followed by *fig* indicate an illustrated figure; followed by *t* indicate a table.